Introduction

Introducing the ultimate guide to kick-starting your career!

"The Ultimate Guide to Kick Starting your Career" is a comprehensive book series offering expert advice on successfully entering the competitive world of work and building essential skills for long-term success and happiness. This invaluable resource provides school leavers and graduates with the guidance they need to make the most of their next step.

By delving into the topics of Native Genius, Strengths, Behaviour Profiling, Networking, Interviewing and Communication, this book series equips readers with the knowledge and tools necessary to navigate the challenges of starting a career, ensuring a strong foundation for a fulfilling professional journey ahead.

In Book 1: "Hear I Am! How to Unlock Your First Career", we'll guide you through the process of discovering your passions, skills, strengths and values, helping you to choose a natural career path that's right for you.

Book 2: "Look at Me! How to Interview with Impact," provides guidance on how to prepare for and ace any job interview. From researching the company and mastering your body language to storytelling so you make a lasting and positive impression on any potential employer or university.

Gain greater understanding of career options in Book 3 "Which Way Now: How to Navigate your way into the World of Work," a comprehensive guide that covers everything from the future of work and industry sectors to the importance of energising work and the many different career paths available to you.

And finally, Book 4 "Can you Here Me? How to Build Confidence in the Art of Communication," a practical guide that helps you develop your communication skills, including networking, active listening, and interviewing with confidence.

Whether you're a recent graduate, a career changer, or just looking to improve your professional skills, the Flying Start XP series, written by career expert Alex Webb, has everything you need to take your career to the next level. Don't let the competitive job market intimidate you - with our book series, you'll have everything you need to stand out and succeed!

Enjoy. Explore. Engage.

BOOK 1: HERE I AM

How to Unlock Your First Career, discovering your natural strengths, skills and behaviours

Contents

01. Awareness
02. Confidence = Employability
03. Resilience

Introduction

Why are you here?

The world of work is changing rapidly and one day all of you are going to become Chief Executives.

You see up until you complete your education, someone else is the Chief Executive of your life, deciding which country you are born in, what sort of house you live in, the education you receive and so on.

But one day... in the not-so-distant future, (if it hasn't happened already), you will become self-reliant.

Now at that point, you may be:

- employed by someone else (e.g., a small start-up local business or maybe a global company)
- self-employed, (e.g., a graphic artist or musician or gardener,)
- running your own business (e.g., photograph or human-technology integration specialist)
- maybe the not-for-profit sector (e.g., a drone manager, fund-raiser, or aid worker)
- perhaps you work in the public sector, you are in HM Forces or the NHS

- or you might become an academic, following your research interests?

But you will have chosen and made your own path.

So how do you start building that path? What direction should you take?
- Straight into work?
- Further studying?
- An Apprenticeship or a Degree Apprenticeship?
- A year out?
- A Graduate Programme?

At Flying Start XP, our focus is to enable employability; we help you unlock your native genius so you can succeed in the world of work. Since our foundation in 2016, our belief has been that if you know more about yourself, your natural strengths, and what's important to you – what makes your heart sing, this is the key to unlocking your next steps and to finding and securing the right role for you.

Whether you are at school, at university or starting your business career, our courses and coaching unlock your natural potential and set you firmly on the path to career success. We are delighted to be bringing you this content in a series of e-books, to learn and explore at a pace that suits you.

Start With The End In Mind

By the end of this book, you will have the

understanding and knowledge to be confident in **who you are** and **what you do**, so you can be confident and proactive in taking your next steps.

To make the most of this book, we thoroughly suggest you use a new notebook or create an online folder so you can keep everything in one place: the outcomes of the exercises, the learnings, the commitments, and anything else that springs to mind as you are reading.

Enjoy our FSXP 'How To' series supporting more young adults who want successful and happy working lives.

Book 1: Here I Am: How to Unlock Your First Career. Discovering your natural strengths, skills, and behaviours. For School Leavers and Graduates

Book 2: Look at Me! How to Interview with Impact. For School Leavers and Graduates

Book 3: Which Way Now? How to Navigate Your Way into the World of Work.
For School Leavers and Graduates

Book 4: Can You Hear Me? How to Build Confidence in the Art of Communication.
For School Leavers and Graduates

Take this opportunity to challenge yourself, reflect and act.

Enjoy!

Alex

Testimonial

"When exploring the world of self-improvement, it can be a difficult task to find a company that not only has the knowledge and ability to aid your development but also one that truly cares about its client, and I can safely say that Flying Start is that needle in the haystack."
Graduate. 1:1 Coaching

Chapter 1 | Your Native Genius

What Is Native Genius?

At Flying Start XP we have a passion for helping young people to find their...

"Native Genius"

We know that everyone in the world has a unique set of different gifts, which means that every single one of you has that Native Genius too. Something that only you have the potential to bring to the world.

You might have seen glimmers of it already – perhaps it's a dexterity with numbers, or an ability to care, to connect easily and effortlessly with other people, or maybe your ability to think three-dimensionally, or to think deeply about solving a problem and to generate highly innovative and creative solutions.

> *"A native genius is something that people do, not only exceptionally well, but absolutely naturally. They do it easily (without extra effort) and freely (without condition) ... they get results that are head-and-shoulders above others, but they do it without breaking a sweat."*

From Multipliers by Liz Wiseman. US researcher, speaker, and author

So where do you start when you are looking for your Native Genius?

You can ask yourself the following questions:
• What do I most enjoy doing? At work and at home?
• Which tasks make my eyes light up?
• What work would I do even if I wasn't being paid for it.?
• When I'm doing this, I don't notice time passing, I am 'in flow' – when does that happen?
• Which of the tasks that I do, would I not like to be given to someone else?

Recruiters have long known the importance of key skills and competencies but are now also using strengths–based interviews to select the best candidate. Merely having the correct qualifications is not enough. You need to prove that you have the required 'Native Genius' for the role.

Story

At FSXP we work in the corporate world with many different organisations and will frequently ask the new arrivals about the recruitment and selection process they underwent in order to get the job.

A new project manager, George, told us that the company he was interested in working for, had held an assessment centre – no CVs were required, or any previous experience. He just had to turn up on the day, to demonstrate his strengths in person. After performing very well on a variety of project-related tasks and activities, he was given an interview after which he was offered the job.

But let's take a step back to discover how George had been so successful.

He had applied for that job because he had done his research and knew they were seeking the natural strengths that he had, in his case, being ordered and organised, being determined to succeed as well as being able to connect easily with clients and associates.

As the company was looking for exactly that in the assessment centre and he could demonstrate it – he got the job.

And the bonus is that he loves what he is doing.

So, what energises you?

Testimonial

> **"I have superpowers which I didn't realise I had. I thought everyone could do what I do. I now realise this is not true and I'm hugely grateful for this learning."**
> *Undergraduate. 1:1 Coaching.*

Chapter 2 | What Gives You Energy?

What Energises You?

First, let's have a look at your hobbies, the activities you go to that bring you joy.

Activity

In your notebook, have a go at drawing your hobbies.

Anything you do that you enjoy - music, sport, gaming, reading, other activities...

Cover the page with as many stickmen as you can muster or icons that bring to life what you do in your spare time. Don't be afraid to draw them, no one is watching!

Reflection: Why do this exercise?

Look at what you've drawn. What could your hobbies say about you? Why would an employer be interested in knowing about them?

Here is a list of some of the hobbies we regularly see:
- Playing a specific sport / musical instrument
- Connecting with friends
- Gaming
- Going to the cinema/theatre

- Socialising
- Performance / amateur dramatics/singing
- Writing/ reading/ art
- Coding/building websites

Let's say your favourite pastime is snooker. What does that say about your Native Genius? It could show that you can focus easily, you can think ahead, work out a strategy, make a plan and follow through on that.

Or do you write and play your own songs or design album covers for fun? Both of those demonstrate your creativity, that you can generate new ideas and take an idea from concept to reality.

If you use social media to promote your hobby and you enjoy reaching out to the wider world and can readily capture the attention of many followers, might this ability, to generate interest, be something that an employer would find interesting and useful?

How did this exercise help you to understand your Native Genius?

Testimonial

"This session was incredibly welcoming and enjoyable, but above all, extremely valuable. I already feel more confident going ahead, knowing I have experiences from many areas of my life, not just my work experience."
Shivani. Graduate. Impact Workshop

Chapter 3 | Your Expertise

Why Is Knowing Your Skills Important?

We work with top executives, and they are telling us that students are not 'business ready'. (How dare they!) "They often don't have the right skills and if they do, they don't know how to use them in a business setting."

So what are the 'right skills'? What are employers looking for?

Each year, the World Economic Forum shares the top skills that employers are looking for. Here's how the lists have chaged in the last 10 years.

2015
1.   Complex problem solving
2.   Coordinating with others
3.   People management
4.   Critical thinking
5.   Negotiation
6.   Quality control
7.   Service orientation
8.   Decision making
9.   Active listening
10. Creativity

2020
1.   Complex problem solving
2.   Critical thinking

3. Creativity
4. People management
5. Coordinating with others
6. Emotional intelligence
7. Decision making
8. Service orientation
9. Negotiation
10. Adaptability and flexibility

2025
1. Analytical thinking and innovation
2. Active learning and learning strategies
3. Complex problem solving
4. Critical thinking and analysis
5. Creativity, originality, and initiative
6. Leadership and social influence
7. Technology use, monitoring and control
8. Technology design and programming
9. Resilience, stress tolerance and flexibility
10. Reasoning, problem-solving and ideation

Reflection

• What skills have you got already? Pick your top 3 from any of the above.
• What skills have you got and didn't know how to articulate?
• What skills would you like to get?
• What evidence have you got of these skills?
• What stories can you tell to show that you are using or have used these skills in the past?

Testimonial

"The group workshop Alex delivered was invaluable and armed me with tools and techniques to kick-start my career. I have now graduated from university and immediately started a Graduate Scheme, feeling far more confident in knowing and understanding not just my strengths and weaknesses but also those of others. No doubt Alex and Flying Start gave me an edge in job applications but, above all, educated me in my self-development."

Izzy. Graduate. Group Workshop

Chapter 4 | How Self-Aware Are You?

The Importance Of Self Awareness

"Self-Awareness is no longer a luxury, it's a necessity"

In the work we do with leaders, we recognise that the best leaders are self-aware ones. Not only does self-awareness support you at school, university and in the workplace, it also helps you understand who you are and how you react to others and to tasks.

With this knowledge you will:
•	Know the working environments in which you will thrive
•	Know the type of teams you want to work in
•	Know how you contribute to those teams

In this chapter, we are going to be focusing on your Behaviour Preferences using
a tool called C-M™

The Aim of C-ME™ is to:
•	Understand Self
•	Understand Others
•	Adapt behaviour to improve relationships

We know that you draw upon different behaviours

depending on **who you're with** (your mates, your family, your colleagues), **the situation** (exams, dinners, interviews, religious settings) and **the level of challenge** (pressure) you face. You will naturally draw upon different behaviours, so you perform well within those scenarios.

C-Me™ does not put you in a box, it gives you some language and understanding to discover how you naturally behave and how that can change depending on the situation.

C-Me™ derives from the work done by psychologist Carl Jung, from which many personality tests come, such as Myers Briggs Type Indicator (MBTI™), Insights Discovery™ and DISC™. C-Me™ is the next generation of colour profiling and we love it. It's colourful, simple, and fast to understand. AND it doesn't put you in a BOX!

Let's start building your self-awareness.

Activity

This or That

Here's a simple activity for you, to start building awareness.

When answering the questions below, think about you at work or volunteering or with your family. Whichever scenario you pick, keep thinking of that scenario all the way through.

Imagine you are standing on a line and for every

set of statements below, you take one step to the left or to the right, dependent on the statement that relates to you the most. Once you have worked through the five sets of statements, where do you end up? To the left of where you started or the right? Maybe you've ended up back in the middle?

*You can also do this exercise by putting your fists out and for every question, hold out a finger on that hand depending on the statement that relates to you the most.

Statement 1
Step Left - I have a small circle of friends
Step Right - I have a large circle of friends

Statement 2
Step left - I prefer to think things through before responding
Step Right - I'm good at responding to things quickly

Statement 3
Step Left - I am better at listening
Step Right - I am better at responding

Statement 4
Step Left - In a group situation I prefer to wait to find out what other people think before giving my views
Step Right - In a group situation I like to get my ideas on the table as soon as possible

Statement 5
Step Left - If I spend the whole day with lots of people, I am exhausted and need time on my own

to recover when I get home

Step Right

If I spend the whole day with lots of people, I am energised and want to talk about it when I get home

So where have you ended up? To the left or the right of where you started?

Extroversion V Reflection

Now for some theory.

Jung's first dichotomy is between Extroversion and Reflection. You will have heard the word Introversion as the opposite of Extroversion. With C-Me™ we prefer to use the word 'Reflection'.

Jung could see that some people were more outward-focused, and some were more inward focussed. For a full understanding of our C-Me™ Chapter, head to www.flyingstartxp.com to purchase our complete book including full colour and images

Extroverted Preference
- Action Orientated
- Outward Focus
- Breadth
- Outspoken
- Bold

Reflective Preference
- Observant
- Inward Focus

- Depth
- Thoughtful
- Cautious

The key thing to remember here, as well as the above description:

- If you have a **high extroverted preference**, you will get your energy from other people. You need to be with others, connect with and communicate with others to restore your energy. If you are shut away, working on your own for too long, you can lose a lot of momentum and we won't see them at your best. You are a solar panel; you need energy from outside of you, to recharge you.

- If you have a **high reflective preference**, you will get your energy from an inward focus, from having that time to reflect and recoup – so time on your own is an OK place for you. You are a battery, you can re-charge yourself.

*Remember that you behave differently depending on who you're with, the situation and the level of challenge or stress. You will be moving up and down this line all the time. You will have a preference though i.e., a starting point from which you will adapt.

Activity

This or That

Here's a simple activity for you, to continue building awareness.

When answering the questions below, think about you at work or volunteering or with your family. Whichever scenario you pick, keep thinking of that scenario all the way through.

Imagine you are standing on a line and for every set of statements below, you take one step to the left or to the right, dependent on the statement that relates to you the most. Once you have worked through the five sets of statements, where do you end up? To the left of where you started or the right? Maybe you've ended up back in the middle?

*You can also do this exercise by putting your fists out and for every question, hold out a finger on that hand depending on the statement that relates to you the most.

Statement 1
Step Left - When making a decision, I like to analyse the pros and cons and use logic to make the decision, firstly
Step Right - When I make a decision, I am concerned with the values and what is best for the people involved, firstly

Statement 2
Step Left - I am more swayed by an argument that is presented logically
Step Right - I am more swayed by an argument that is presented sincerely

Statement 3
Step Left - I like to be recognised for what I have done
Step Right - I like to be appreciated for who I am

Statement 4
Step Left - When feeding back on someone else's performance or presentation, I tend to start with what is wrong, missing, or inconsistent
Step Right - When feeding back on someone else's performance or presentation, I tend to start with what was good about it

Statement 5
Step Left - I make decisions with my head and want to be fair
Step Right - I make decisions with my heart and want to be compassionate and consider other people's feelings.

So where have you ended up? To the left or the right of where you started?

Thinking V Feeling

Back to the theory

Jung's second dichotomy looks at how we make our decisions. With our head or with our heart?

Thinking Preference
- Analytical
- Objective
- Task Orientated
- Correct

- Strong-minded

Feeling Preference
- Personal
- Considerate
- Involved
- Subjective
- Relationship-orientated
- Accommodating

We know that decisions are made with both head and heart. You will do one, firstly.

Now you will have an idea of whether you are:

- **Extroverted / Thinker**
- **Extroverted/ Feeling**
- **Reflective /Feeling**
- **Reflective Thinking**

What does this mean? Let's have a look at the behaviours associated with each of the colours.

How many statements from each of the colours resonate with you?

- RED - **Extroverted / Thinker**

o   Confident and optimistic
o   Task focused
o   Enjoys stretching goals
o   Leads from the front
o   Sets a winning mentality
o   Thinks big
o   Direct and to the point

- YELLOW - **Extroverted/ Feeling**

o   Free-spirited
o   Friendly and optimistic
o   Enjoys networking opportunities
o   Inspirational and visionary
o   Lively, sociable and fun
o   Not afraid to take risks
o   Spontaneous and imaginative

- GREEN - **Reflective /Feeling**

o   Considerate
o   Concern for colleagues
o   Avoids conflict
o   Involves others in decisions
o   Respects others' values
o   Supportive and loyal
o   Works for a democratic solution

- BLUE - **Reflective Thinking**

o   Logical and analytical
o   Enjoys problem-solving
o   Needs time for reflection
o   Realistic
o   Sorts out the details
o   Strong sense of duty
o   Structured and disciplined

Which statements relate to you?
What's your blend of colours?
Why don't you build a graph of colours by adding
a colour block for every statement you agree with?

Final Notes

As human beings, we are a blend of all colours, we have to be. Never put yourself in a box. Using C-Me™ colours, allows you to understand the 4 colours separately which helps you begin to understand other people's blends. You can then react to them in a way that supports them rather than frustrates them.

What happens to your behaviours on a Good Day? Which statements relate to you? What is your blend?

- RED - **Extroverted Feeling**

o   Bold, determined &decisive
o   Drives hard for delivery
o   Plays to win
o   Focuses on results
o   Powerful advocate
o   Enjoys a challenge

- YELLOW – **Extroverted Feeling**

o   Energetic and enthusiastic
o   Positive outlook
o   Embraces change
o   Sociable and outgoing
o   Generous and open-minded
o   A real zest for life
o   Sees the bright side

- GREEN - **Reflective Feeling**

o   Tactful and diplomatic
o   Dedicated to the team

o   Works until the job is done
o   Kind and considerate
o   Tolerant and open-minded
o   Can see both sides
o   Steady and reliable

- BLUE - **Reflective Thinking**

o   Realistic
o   Focuses on details
o   Considers all the facts
o   Strong work ethic
o   Brings clarity to complexity
o   Gets the facts in place
o   Sticks to principles

For a full understanding of our C-Me™ Chapter, head to www.flyingstartxp.com to purchase our complete book including full colour and images

What happens to your behaviours on a Bad Day? Which statements relate to you? What is your blend of colours?

- RED - **Extroverted Thinking**

o   Only results matter
o   Can be controlling
o   Rocks the boat
o   Short fuse
o   Can be intolerant
o   May not be listening
o   Action overrides planning

- YELLOW - **Extroverted Thinking**

- o   Energetic and enthusiastic
- o   May miss details
- o   Can appear disorganised
- o   Jumps between ideas
- o   All talk no action
- o   Lax time management
- o   Everything to excess
- o   Inclined to talk too much

- • GREEN - **Reflective Thinking**

- o   Appears to lack urgency
- o   Can be indecisive
- o   Often self-critical
- o   Procrastinates
- o   Reluctant to change
- o   Setting priorities is difficult
- o   Constantly checking consensus

- • BLUE - **Reflective Thinking**

- o   Emotionally detached
- o   Hypercritical
- o   Obsessive about the detail
- o   Slow to trust
- o   Undemonstrative
- o   Lacks spontaneity
- o   Constrained by the rules

Further Reading

Book: 'Surrounded by Idiots – The Four Types of Human Behaviour (i.e., How to Understand Those Who Cannot be Understood) by Thomas Erikson

C-Me™ Reports

Go to **www.tlrdynamics.com/c-me-report/** to purchase your own C-Me™ Report.

Our Youth Reports are £39, and they will show your:

- Position on the C-Me™ Wheel
- Your colour blends for your Adapted (You when you put a mask on) and your Natural Behaviours
- An Overview
- Resilient Strengths
- Areas of Development
- Communication Needs
- Contribution to a Team

Testimonial

"I have felt that I was missing something when it came to applying for jobs, missing an unknown key ingredient to starting a successful career. The course showed me that ingredient was understanding myself. Using a wide range of techniques over a fun and engaging couple of days, you really do gain an insight about what employers are looking for but also how you can see yourself to them. After attending I can now say that I have found my colour, I have found myself and now I can find my future."
Robert. Young Adult. 2-day Future Leaders Programme (Prince's Trust)

If you'd like to know more about C-Me™ colours

and how you can use it to support you with your next steps, your personal statements or learning how to best interact with others:

- Book a 1:1 Coaching Session
- Book a Group coaching session
- Head to www.flyingstartxp.com to purchase other complete colour and image-filled books from our website.

Application Story

Meet Ahmed and Dionne

Ahmed and Dionne are both tasked with an assignment during the start of their new roles, they have to present back to their team about a company topic. Dionne leads with Red, and Ahmed leads with Green.

By knowing who you are and how you behave, it's so much easier to understand why you react in the way you do, why you have certain clashes with certain staff or colleagues you just can't seem to get on with – well it's probably because you have a different colour energy and therefore do things in a different way.

It might be tempting to use this information in a way that says – 'I'm red so this is how I behave. Deal with it!' But that's just an excuse. Instead, you could use your knowledge of colours to ensure a better outcome for both parties and dial your colour behaviours down or up depending on the situation.

Ahmed leads with Green, he is considerate, warm, loyal, supportive, conflict avoidant and concerned for others' feelings

Dionne leads with Red, she is determined, confident, direct, keen to set a winning mentality

1.   What do you think happened?

Ahmed may be thinking "Why is she putting me under so much pressure? Is Dionne really listening to my ideas?"

Dionne may be thinking "Why isn't Ahmed enthused with my ideas? Doesn't he want to win this pitch?"

2.   What would happen if they were armed with C-Me™ tools

Ahmed will think "I will be more proactive in putting my thoughts across"

Dionne will think "I will be more aware of my tendency to take over and will listen to others' ideas more"

Reflection

- The more you know about yourself and where you are on the colour wheel, the better choices you can make about the type of career you would be suited for. **(See Book 3: Which Way Now? – www.flyingstartxp.com)**

- Now you know a little more about who

you are and your behaviour preferences, what are your 3 key learnings?

· Write them in your notebook.

Testimonial

'C-Me colour profiling is fantastic, the accuracy is scary and for me, from now on, an absolute necessity for us.'
Harry Spear. Director. Caribbean Elective. Director. Impact Workshop (Awareness)

Chapter 5 | What are your Top 3 Strengths?

What Are Your Strengths

The past two chapters have helped you identify your strengths, whether they are strengths that your behaviour preference offers or strengths from the skills that you have.

If you are asked, following the last two chapters 'What Are your Top 3 strengths?' What would you reply?

Having the answer to this question is key. Having that awareness of what you bring to an organisation, a role or a team means you can talk more confidently about yourself. You now have some language that you can use to be able to articulate those strengths too.

Organisations will spend a lot of money on people knowing their strengths. Imagine how impressive it would be if you arrived already knowing them!

Companies know that when people know and use their strengths, they are more productive, they are more engaged, they stay with the company longer, they take less time off – they are happier, and the companies are more successful as a result.

Think of a jigsaw. When you see a job description, it's a company looking for that missing piece. This piece needs to be of a certain shape and size. It's the same with the role. The company will be looking for certain strengths and skills. The more you know about yours, the better decisions you can make as to whether a job is suitable for you. You can start to think – is this job going to allow me to use my native genius, my natural set of skills and behaviour strengths?

Reflection

Think about the following and write your answers in your notebook:

- What it's like when you are using your strengths – how does it feel?
- When did you last use any of those strengths? What were you doing?
- If you could just use these all day, what would it be like?
- If you had to use different skills that you are less familiar with, what might that be like?

Summary

Remember

> *"ORGANISATIONS NEED PEOPLE*
> *WHO KNOW THEIR STRENGTHS."*

Knowing yours will make you more employable

and make it easier for you to find a role you will enjoy!

If you want to know how to successfully bring your strengths to life through storytelling, look out for our book 2, **Look at Me! How to Interview with Impact**

Testimonial

"Whilst incredibly enjoyable, this programme equips you with the skills to perform in an interview and create and tailor a perfect CV, as well as being able to pin down your interests to coax you in the right direction for the future you want. Most importantly, the course helps you discover, embrace, and harness your skills in order for you to accentuate these traits so you can use them to your greatest possible advantage! I would recommend to anybody who has the opportunity to be involved."
Libby. Pupil. 3-day Future Leaders Programme

Chapter 6 | Knowing your Compass

Introduction

So far within this book all about your Native Genius, we have focused on your hobbies, your skills, your behaviours and your strengths.

We're now going a little deeper.

A chance to look at what underlines all our behaviour and the things that guide us through our lives.

Our Values.

If you think of an iceberg. Above the water line is what people see and this is how people will judge us. They will judge us mainly by what we do and how we act, our behaviours. Our values sit underneath the water line. People won't see them unless they do a deep dive.

'Personal values' are the general expression of what is most important to you and, like the compass, they guide you in your life.

- That might be respect – that everyone treats each other kindly
- Or it might be competition – so that everyone is striving to do their best
- Appreciation is important and you couldn't work somewhere where your

hard work went unnoticed
- Or it might be freedom – without that you feel constrained and unable to be creative.

But for everyone, these values are completely different.

> **"Values are like fingerprints. Nobody's are the same, but you leave 'em all over everything you do."**
> Elvis Presley

When you are choosing a career path, it is crucial that you examine whether your values fit those of the organisation you are considering.

Activity

Lots of things could be important to us but we know it's a value when someone treads all over them, it may feel like a kick in the stomach. If your value is respect, then someone dropping litter on the floor could really anger you because they're not respecting the environment, other people, and the general tidiness of a place.

Or if appreciation is of high value, you may have a high need for being thanked, for having your work noticed, for people being grateful. Remember back to one of the C-Me statements – 'I like to be more appreciated for who I am' rather than 'Recognised for what I have done'.

Below is a list of values, take some time to simply read through the list, marking those values that are important to you.

List Of Values

Use the list of values to stimulate your thinking and create new inner connections OR for a more in-depth activity to find your Core Values, try out our online Values tool created by our sister company TLRdynamics Ltd in partnership with Resilient Leaders Elements which gives you an option of 100 values, each one comes with a description too. It's a FREE tool. Head to **www.tlrdynamics.com/coach/fsxp/**

Abundance
Acceptance
Achievement
Adventure
Aesthetics
Appreciation
Authenticity
Balance
Beauty
Bliss
Caring
Career
Cheerfulness
Clarity
Commitment
Compassion
Co-operation
Confidence
Contentment
Courage

Creativity
Daring
Dedication
Detachment
Determination
Devotion
Diligence
Discipline
Discernment
Discrimination
Empathy
Empowerment
Energy
Enthusiasm
Excellence
Faith
Family
Fame
Flexibility
Forgiveness
Freedom
Friendship
Fun
Generosity
Goodwill
Grace
Gratitude
Growth
Happiness
Harmlessness
Harmony
Healing
Health

Honesty
Hope
Humility
Inclusiveness
Insight
Integrity
Influence
Intelligence
Intimacy
Introspection
Intellectual growth
Intuition
Joy
Justice
Kindness
Knowledge
Leadership
Learning
Love
Loyalty
Maturity
Money
Openness
Order
Passion
Patience
Peace
Positive
Power
Prosperity
Purity
Purpose
Recognition

Relationships
Respect
Reverence
Sacrifice
Security
Serenity
Service
Sharing
Silence
Spirituality
Spontaneity
Strength
Status
Support
Surrender
Success
Tolerance
Trust
Trustworthiness
Truth
Understanding
Union
Unity
Wisdom
Winning
Wealth

Reflection

- Now you know a little more about your values, what does that tell you about you?
- How does this knowledge help you?
- How can you use this knowledge to

support your future?

- How do your values connect with your C-Me™ colours and the behaviours you show?

Testimonial

"Knowing my values was a key learning for me. It made me realise that I was in the wrong environment because I wasn't able to live them. It made me feel like I wasn't good at my Saturday job. I have now left and found a job which suits me better. It's made such a huge difference and my confidence is coming back. I can't thank Alex enough for this realisation."
Student. 1:1 Coaching

Chapter 7 | Conclusions & Reflections

"Reflection – Looking back so the view looking forward is even clearer"
Unknown

Reflection

I know that some of you will have seen the word 'Reflection' and thought about moving on. If we lead with high extroversion, our need to go fast could stop us from reflecting and therefore maximising our learning.

'When F1 cars are in a race, they slow down as they enter a bend, this means they can accelerate out of the bend still in control. Sometimes we need to slow down so that we can go fast.'

When working with young adults, we can see how the different colour preferences approach reflection. So here are some questions that may support you.

So What?

What have you learnt? Write these in your notebook.

What 3 things stand out to you from reading Chapters 1 to 5 that have interested you?

A CHANCE TO PRACTICE: Who Am I?

Let's practice using some of your newly learned language.

Now you know your skills, strengths, behaviour preferences and your values, how would you describe yourself?

Here are a few examples

'I am enthusiastic, empathetic and have a love for life. I enjoy working with others and coming up with lots of ideas. Respect, honesty and having fun are really important to me.'

'I am a logical, analytical problem solver. I enjoy independent learning and getting into the detail of an issue. My love of chess allows me to use my strengths in a competitive environment too. Determination, hard work and intellectual growth are important to me.'

Application

By writing your own sentences:
- You will have the words to use when someone asks you about your strengths or what you enjoy
- You now have awareness of how you contribute to a team
- You now have greater confidence and self-belief in what you can offer

How are you going to use this knowledge?
- Personal Statements
- CV's
- Cover Letters
- Linkedin
- Interviews

CHALLENGE – A CHANCE TO WIN A FREE C-ME™™ REPORT

For anyone who emails me their final sentence, they will be put into a quarterly drawer to win a C-Me Report for themselves or a family member.

Email your sentence to **hello@flyingstartxp.com**

Final Quote

> **"Don't ask what the world needs. Ask what makes you come alive... What the world needs is people who have come alive".**
> *Howard Thurman, Philosophy
> and Civil Rights Leader*

Testimonial

> **"I would like to thank you for the work you have done for me and hope you can continue to positively impact the future of many bright, young, and aspirational people!"**
> *Dale. Graduate. 5-day Future Leaders Programme*

BOOK TWO: LOOK AT ME

How to Interview with Impact

Contents

01. Awareness
02. Confidence = Employability
03. Resilience

Introduction

Why Are You Here?

I wonder why you're reading this book. Is it because you've been told to by a parent? Or maybe a teacher or a lecturer has recommended it? Or maybe you have done your
own research and found this book because you're wanting to build the skills that will put you in the best possible position when starting to look for a job.

If this is you, then congratulations. You're already showing up, showing that you are proactively engaging with ways to make you a stronger candidate, a more aware individual and someone who wants to learn.

At Flying Start XP, our focus is to enable employability. We help you unlock your Native Genius so you can succeed in the world of work. Since our foundation in 2016, we believe that if you know more about yourself, your natural strengths, what's important to you and what makes your heart sing, this is the key to unlocking your next steps and to finding and securing the right role for you.

Whether you are at school, at university or

starting your business career, our courses and coaching unlock your natural potential and set you firmly on the path to career success. And now we're bringing you this content in a series of Books. This way we can reach more young adults who want successful and happy working lives.

At Flying Start XP we know that everyone in the world has a unique set of different gifts, which means that every single one of you has their own Native Genius - something that only you have the potential to bring to the world. How do you then ensure that others can see your potential and fully understand the value you can bring?

We hope you have already read Book 1: Here I Am, as this will have given you a great insight into understanding your Native Genius. Knowing your hobbies, your skills, your behaviour preferences and your values can help you to appreciate the:

- strengths you have
- environments in which you will thrive
- types of work that will energise you.

If you haven't read this book, head to 'Hear I Am: How to Unlock Your First Career' Book 1 in our FSXP Book series.

Our focus in this book is on how you start to tell your story. How you can showcase your skills in an interview and be able to articulate them in a way that is well thought through, that will help you stand out and be remembered.

We want to prepare you so you can step confidently into your next job interview, with the advantage of having learnt and practised effective interview preparation tools and techniques, enabling you to stand out above the crowd.

We believe that 'Interviewing with Impact' is all about the preparation so let's make a start.

Start With The End In Mind

By the end of this book, you will have the understanding and knowledge to be confident in who you are and what you do, so you can be proactive, confident and articulate when preparing, practising and performing in an interview.

To make the most of this book, we thoroughly suggest you use a new notebook or create an online folder to keep everything in one place: the outcomes of the exercises, the learnings, the commitments, and anything else that springs to mind as you are reading this book. If you're planning on reading our whole series, keeping everything in one place will make it so much easier to find.

Book 1: Here I Am: How to Unlock Your First Career. Discovering your natural strengths, skills, and behaviours. For School Leavers and Graduates

Book 2: Look at Me! How to Interview with Impact. For School Leavers and Graduates

Book 3: Which Way Now? How to Navigate Your Way into the World of Work. For School Leavers and Graduates

Book 4: Can You Hear Me? How to Build Confidence in the Art of Communication. For School Leavers and Graduates

Take this opportunity to challenge yourself, reflect and act.

Enjoy!

Alex

Testimonial

"This workshop not only helped me improve my interview technique but also helped improve my confidence. Too often I've fallen at the last hurdle all because I was too nervous to do myself credit. I now have the tools and techniques to maximise my opportunities."
Student: Interview Coaching

Chapter 1 | Who am I?
What do I have offer?

What! More Skills!

At Flying Start XP we have a passion for helping young people to find their...

In Book 1: Here I Am, we focused on your Native Genius, what you have to offer the world. Sometimes, we don't appreciate our own strengths. We may believe that everyone can do what we do. But they can't. And sometimes we need to remind ourselves of that.

By understanding your values, your behaviour preferences, your skills, and strengths, you will start to understand how you differ from your friends and family members.

What you find easy and what brings you energy may be completely different from that which energises someone else. Remember the jigsaw piece in Book 1: Here I Am.

We all have our own shape, and we need to find a role or an organisation which needs this shape.

In addition to understanding our values, behaviours, skills, and strengths, it's also important to recognise other areas of our lives which could be of interest in an interview. Things that often we leave out or we don't think are important. The areas of our lives which make us us, which makes us human.

- What do I most enjoy doing? At work and at home?
- Which tasks make my eyes light up?
- What work would I do even if I wasn't being paid?
- When I'm doing this, I don't notice time passing, I am 'in flow'. When does that happen?
- Which of the tasks that I do, would I not like to be given to someone else?

Recruiters have long known the importance of key skills and competencies, but are now also using strengths–based interviews to select the best candidate. Merely having the correct qualifications is not enough. You need to prove that you have the required 'Native Genius' for the role.

Some Interesting You Facts

In our workshops, we ask our participants to stand in a circle and to take a step forward if they answer yes to any of the following questions.

- Who can speak more than one language?
- Who has travelled to more than five countries?
- Who is the older sibling?

- Who loves reading?
- Who can use sign language to speak to a blind and/or deaf person?
- Who has saved a life?
- Who can make people laugh?
- Who feels strongly about climate change?
- Who has personally raised more than £200 for charity?
- Whose family lives in another country?
- Who wants to run their own business?
- Who has climbed a mountain?
- Who has been to a dangerous country?
- Who enjoys dancing?
- Who has been to a festival?

As people step forward, we ask, 'Why would that be interesting to an employer?'

Let's take playing a musical instrument as an example. That would demonstrate that you are dedicated, focused, able to learn, able to practice, perhaps have experienced overcoming the nerves of exams or being out of your comfort zone, or if you are self-taught, the commitment to self-improvement.

All of these are important and useful skills within the workplace.

How about being an older sibling?'

This can show patience, leadership, being a role model, being caring and supportive and the willingness to take responsibility.

Now look again at those questions, this time making a note of what each of your answers could demonstrate to an employer.

- Who can speak more than one language?
- Who has travelled to more than five countries?
- Who is the older sibling?
- Who loves reading?
- Who can use sign language to speak to a deaf person?
- Who has saved a life?
- Who can make people laugh?
- Who feels strongly about climate change?
- Who has personally raised more than £200 for charity?
- Whose family lives in another country?
- Who wants to run their own business?
- Who has climbed a mountain?
- Who has been to a dangerous country?
- Who enjoys dancing?
- Who has been to a festival?

As you consider each of these questions, see if you can remember any stories related to them which show your key strengths. If you haven't already done so, make a list of your key strengths and make sure that you have a story to tell for each one. You will need these for exercises later in the book.

So What?

Remember, the more stories you can tell about the things you have done, the more an employer will understand the skills you can bring and your attitude to work.

Testimonial

"Finding out how to show off my skills and give the right evidence was a real eye-opener. Much easier once I knew how."
School Student.

Chapter 2 | Prove it

By Now, You Should Have A Solid List Of Your Strengths, Skills And Values, Written In Your Notebooks From Book 1. But, Do You Have Proof? Do You Have The Evidence?

Evidence gives you the stories that show your interviewer your strengths, your skills, your experiences and your Native Genius.

How can you bring these strengths to life, articulating them in a way they become memorable and impactful when you're next in an interview?

Activity: Brainstorm

Let's start with a quick brainstorm.

What experiences have you had at school/university, through work experience or volunteering where you could find some good stories to showcase your strengths?

Write down as many things as possible. Below are some ideas to support you:

- Volunteering
- Duke of Edinburgh
- Fundraising
- Musical Groups

- Sports Teams
- Prefect
- Travelling in this country or abroad
- Any jobs (paid or unpaid)
- Blogging or vlogging
- Being a Carer
- Young Enterprise
- Guides / Scouts / Cadets

Your Strengths

Step 1

From your list of strengths, whether that be from your list of skills or the strengths that come from your C-Me™ Behaviour preferences, see Book 1, pick three that you know you do effortlessly.

Write those three down.

Step 2

Now it's time to think about the best stories you have, that highlight you using that particular strength. From your list of experiences, you've just written down, which
experience gives you the best evidence of that strength?

Here are some examples

- Strength is Creativity. The experience is: At school / University, I directed a play
- Strength is Collaboration. The experience is: I started a new charity with a few of my

friends

- Strength is Detail-orientated. The experience is: I set up several spreadsheets to make it easier for stock control when working with the local greengrocer.

You may even have more than one story that connects with your strengths. Keep writing them down. You can then choose the best story – The story that works the hardest for you.

Let's take Creativity as an example. What experiences do we have that show our creativity......

CREATIVITY – Directing a play; creating social media blogs for a charity event; YouTub'ing; Winning an award for creative writing; Young Enterprise innovation.

Why Spent Time Working Out My Evidence?

We know that when you're under pressure, your prefrontal cortex, which uses logic to solve problems, works less well and this results in cloudy thinking.

Some of you may have heard of T-Cup, (Thinking Correctly Under Pressure). It's a phrase we first heard from Sir Clive Woodward, who coached the England Rugby team. This team trained and practised for every eventuality they could imagine. This practise allowed them to think clearly and correctly under pressure. In the final of The Rugby World Cup in 2003, that tactic proved invaluable. After going into extra time, they were able to hold their nerve and set up a move which allowed Johnny Wilkinson to kick a drop goal, winning the match! The whole team knew, at least 5 moves previously to this drop goal, what the sequence of play was to be. They became World Champions because of their ability to think correctly under pressure.

And that is exactly what you will want to be doing when you are sitting in front of your interviewer or perhaps an interview panel. The more time you spend working through your evidence and practising with great examples and stories of how you've used your strengths and skills, the more you will be able to talk about them confidently in an interview.

If you know what's coming, you can prepare for it.

Testimonial

"I would recommend this relaxed but professional workshop as it is at a more advanced level than others I've seen. Alex and Charlie bring a wealth of knowledge and link well to their real-life experiences in business and education."
Careers Coordinator. Downs School

Chapter 3 | Tell Me a Story

Introduction

How often do you worry about waffling at an interview?

We're now going to give you a tool to help bring your evidence to life and to help you be concise. It's called the STAR Technique

Star Stands For:

SITUATION: Briefly identify the SITUATION – When, Where, Who, With?

TASK: What was the TASK or problem?

ACTION: Detail your specific ACTION. What did you do? How did you do it?

RESULT: Describe the RESULTS.

Outcomes, savings, accomplishments.

Activity: Brainstorm

You can use STAR to describe an everyday situation such as getting up in the morning.

What was the:-

Situation? This morning after breakfast

Task? I had to brush my teeth

Action? I used my pink toothbrush and paste and used an up-and-down motion for two minutes

Result? My teeth were clean and my mouth was fresh and minty.

We can use the STAR technique for anything. Here's another example – this time let's use the strength of being proactive.

Situation: Friends wanted to raise money for Children in Need

Task: We decided to organise a disco

Action: I put it out on social media and then followed up by selling tickets with friends outside of school

Result: 200 people attended and we raised £500.

This time let's add another 'R' at the end. This final 'R' stands for Reflection.

Reflection: I learnt that social media when used well can really support communication and is brilliant for raising money.

By using this method, you get to the facts quickly as well as sharing a memorable story.

Using the STARR technique means:
- You can be brief and impactful
- You get to share more stories
- You share the results and the reflection which shows greater awareness

If you are chatty, the STARR technique also allows you to use 'the Results and
Reflection' as a break and to 'stop talking'.

Strengthening Your Starr Story

Now it's your turn. In your notebooks, your challenge is to write a STARR story for each of your top three strengths.

Remember: Use a different experience to demonstrate each strength. What is your best example of each one? Which stories will make you more memorable?

This can be tough so, as you're writing your script, practise it out loud. How does it sound? Am I being succinct, am I getting the story across? Am I painting a strong picture for my interviewer to really understand my story?

Testimonial

"This course was simply invaluable. It allowed me to understand the key skills required for Interviews. The opportunity to put these into practice during the course, including a practice interview for a University Degree or Job Preference for the future was extremely beneficial. Both Alex and Charlie delivered an exceptional session; it really is worthwhile if you'd like to learn the fundamental techniques and preparation tips that will allow you to fulfil your potential and improve your employability in the modern world."
Sixth Former. Impact Workshop.
Interviewing with Impact

Chapter 4 | Is This The Right Job for You?

What Makes A Job The Right Job?

In this chapter, we are simply gifting you a template which you can use for every job interview you have coming up, wherever you are in your career.

This template can help you analyse a job description, so you can research:

- Exactly what skills and strengths the role requires, which means that you can check whether they match your skills and strengths
- The type of company it is, and the opportunities and culture offered
- What questions they could ask you, so you can prepare your answers
- Questions you can ask at interview to fill in the gaps in your knowledge about the role and organisation

All you need now is to find a job description that you can test this out on OR a job you're looking at interviewing for.

Step 1
In your notebooks, on a full page, draw quadrants.

In quadrant one (top left) write: What skills, behaviours or experience are they looking for?

In quadrant two (top right) write: What information do they give about the organisation/ course?

In quadrant three (bottom right) write: What else do I want to know about the organisation?

In quadrant four (bottom left): What other skills, behaviours or experience do I have?

Step 2

In Quadrant One: From what you see on the job description, what are the skills, behaviours or experiences the company is looking for? You may have to read between the lines. For example, if the job role mentions working in a fast-moving environment, they are probably looking for someone flexible, agile and able to make quick decisions.

List them all down.

Now highlight the ones that appear in your list of strengths and skills. Do they match?

If enough of them match, this could be a good job for you. If there are only a few matches, this may not be a job in which you will thrive. Time to look elsewhere.

Step 3

From your list of skills, behaviours, and strengths, now it's your chance to think about the types of questions they might ask you to find out if you have the right skills.

For example:
If 'collaboration' was a key skill they were looking for, the question could be 'Give me an example of a time when you were collaborative'

Because you know this is coming, you will have prepared a great STARR story that shows strong evidence of a time when you were 'collaborative'.

This question could be used for all the skills. You don't have to have a STARR story for each one because if you have a strong STARR story, it may showcase more than one strength or skill. Ensure you have the best stories ready, showcasing you at your best.

Step 4

In Quadrant Two: Look at what you know about the company or role. In the job description, they may highlight the size of the organisation, their locations, their values, the company mission, and their clients.

This is a chance for you to understand more about the type of company they are and whether it's the right environment for you.

In Book 3: Which Way Now, we share the C-Me™ company wheels of different companies, which provides a greater understanding of the company culture.

So check this book out.

Step 5

In Quadrant Three: Write down what we don't know about the company or role because it hasn't been mentioned in the description. What information are you missing?

The size of the organisation? Their locations? Their values? The company mission? Their clients?

Step 6

Having completed quadrants two and three, we will be able to see some gaps. This is where your research can be focused. What information are you missing?

Now go and find the answers.

Places to look could be:
- The company website
- Linkedin
- Your contacts
- Your networks
- Glass Door: a review site where employees

write their experience of working
- for that company, the best employers to work for etc.
- The news and social media

Start digging and if you can't find out the answers, this could give you a strong question to ask at the end of the interview when they ask if you have any questions for them.

A question could be phrased something like 'I was interested to read on your website about xxx, can you tell me a little more about how that affects the company / how that works / how that…'

Step 7

In Quadrant Four: This is a space for you to write down any of your additional skills. Any strengths or values you have on your list from earlier that haven't been mentioned in the job description?

When you're in an interview and they ask if you have any further questions, this could be your response:

'I know the job description didn't highlight the exact skills of xxx, but I just wanted to let you know that this is one of my key strengths and I believe it can add value to this role because…'

Your confidence and awareness will shine through if you can add this one to your interview.

Step 8

The importance of rehearsing.

Now that you have your STARR stories prepped and ready to go, you've researched the company and you know the questions you're going to ask, it's time to rehearse.

Why bother with rehearsal?

Michael Caine (an experienced actor who has starred in many successful movies) says

"The rehearsal is the work, the performance is the celebration of the work".

In this case the performance = the interview!

Rehearsing will:
- Make you feel more confident
- Help you refine the words you use
- Help you to be succinct
- Confirm your choice of the best example for each skill

Testimonial

"Being in a small group, it was great to have Alex put everything into a personal level and make it specific for each of us. I really enjoyed self-placing myself on the C-Me wheel and then comparing it to my report. Also, being provided with a process and template to prepare for an interview and predict questions and compile answers. I would definitely recommend this course."
Isobel. Student. Group Workshop

Chapter 5 | Questions for Interview

What Are Your Strengths

Here are some simple examples of some of the top questions asked at interviews and
also a few ideas of questions you can ask your interviewers.

Top Questions Asked At Interview

- Tell me about yourself.
- Why do you want to work in this organisation?
- What skills do you think we are looking for?
- What evidence do you have of those skills?
- What are your strengths?
- What are your weaknesses?
- Give me three reasons why you think we should employ you.
- What accomplishments are you most proud of and why?
- Describe a time something went wrong and how you dealt with it.
- What motivates you?
- Have you got any questions for us?

Questions To Ask At The End Of An Interview

Questions about the role
- What would you see as the top priorities in the first few months in this role?
- Could you tell me a little bit about the corporate culture and what kind of employees you consider a good fit?
- I'm keen to find out about opportunities for personal development in this company... what can you tell me about that?
- What do you like most about working for this company?
- What was your career journey into doing this job? What was your background?

Questions about the interview and asking for feedback
- What are the next steps; when do you expect to reach a decision?
- Are you looking to choose the best candidate in the next week or so, or do you
- expect the process to take longer?

Tell Me About Yourself

This question is one of the most popular ways of starting an interview or an informal chat.

Let's think about how we can prepare for

this question ensuring we provide enough information to the interviewer, so they want to ask you further questions about those areas.

Think about your strengths, the things you love doing, your hobbies, your family, and your experiences. We can then break them down into 'Outside of Work' and 'Inside of Work.' Here are some examples:

Outside Work / University / School
- I'm quite reflective, I love reading, I'm passionate about hip hop and do some DJ-ing
- I'm from a large family, I play loads of sports and am very involved in the local community centre

At Work / University / School
- I enjoy data analysis and love problem-solving
- I get lots of satisfaction when I am delivering great customer service and making a difference for other people
- I have a degree in computer sciences and, whilst at University, I spent a lot of time building websites and creating apps with some fellow students which resulted in the university asking us to develop some of our apps further.

When you put it all together, it could sound a lot like this...

'I am currently 18 years old, living in XXXX, working in a local pub as the Assistant Manager, leading a team of 15 people. My background has been quite different to most. I was adopted from the US, growing up in Spain for my earlier years, so my Spanish is proficient. I am an only child, so I've learnt how to be proactive and throw myself in at the deep end. I've grown up playing sport, which I love. I know this has contributed to my ability to work well with others. I love being creative, taking time out to draw is important to me and it also gives me time to think of new ideas.'

When you read the above, think about all the questions the interviewer might want to ask. About their experience running a team, their creativity, their Spanish, their sport and so on.

Or this one:

'I am 25 years old; I live with my parents and have two sisters. I was born in the UK and brought up in Chilli. I went to school there, so I grew up bilingual. I came back to the UK when I was 11, doing my GSCE and A levels in the UK. I went to Uni in Plymouth where I studied Internal Relations and Spanish and did my year out in Valencia studying translation. Once I'd graduated, I worked in the Co-op during the Pandemic and have recently left to start studying for the Makers Academy boot camp to kick-start my career in tech.

I believe my key strengths are critical thinking, common sense, communication, and determination'

If you throw in a few of your strengths to your 'Tell me about Yourself' Statement, the interviewer is likely to ask you more about them.

You are then in control of the interview because they want to know more about you.

Your Turn

What's your 'Tell me about Yourself' answer?

Practice it out loud. Record it on your phone. Watch yourself. Share it with a friend.

The more you practice it, the more it will feel natural, so when your pre-frontal cortex is going a little crazy due to nerves at the start of the interview, you have a way of calming down and settling in.

YOUR CHALLENGE – <u>A Chance to Win a Free C-Me™ Report</u>

For anyone who emails me their 'Tell Me About Yourself' sentence, you will be put into a quarterly drawer to win a C-Me Report for themselves or a family member. We shall also share some feedback to help you make it even better. Email your sentence to hello@flyingstartxp.com

Testimonial

"Despite being confident in my own ability, during the assessment centre, I implemented a wide range of things I learnt whilst on the Flying Start course and am completely sure that they helped me in being offered the job!"
Dale. Graduate. 5-day Future Leaders Programme

Chapter 6 | The Importance of First Impressions

How long does it take to make a good first impression?

According to recent research, it's only about seven seconds. That's not long so let's make sure we get it right.

From the moment you start to interact with a company, there will many opportunities to make a great first impression. That could be through your emails, possibly an online interview, followed by a face-to-face interview.

Everyone you meet along your route to an interview could be a gatekeeper, a person who has a say in whether you get the job or not. So be polite.

Smile at the receptionist, engage in conversation with those in the waiting room, and dress appropriately. These factors may just be the 1% you need to get the job over another candidate.

Note: If you need support in accessing interview wear, check out 'Suited and Booted' and 'Smartworks'. Both UK companies can support job applicants with interview wear.

Top Online Interview Tips

- If you find yourself having an online interview, please remember the points below.
- Find a quiet, private, well-lit place, free from possible interruptions.
- Ensure your internet connection is stable.
- Check that your computer's audio is working.
- Test your computer's webcam.
- Close any unnecessary web browser tabs and applications.
- Dress professionally and avoid bright colours.
- Have a pen, notepad and copy of your CV on your desk.
- When listening, nod and smile to show you are engaged.
- Use hand gestures when appropriate.
- Place your phone in silent mode.
- Consider your background and light. Avoid having a window behind you or any strange artwork or pictures.

What Does Your Body Language Say About You?

In the 1960s, Professor Mehrabian and his team in California were looking at the importance of body language in communication. They focused on what people paid attention to when they were uncertain about a message, or they were meeting them for the first time.

The result was as follows:

- Content, what you say: 7%
- Voice and your tone: 38%
- Body Language and facial expressions: 55%

You may have done lots of work on your STARR stories, you know what you're going to say but the tone and the body language are the things that could make or break the interview.

How can you practice this?

Video STAR

With the luxury of technology, recording yourself answering interview questions will give you an idea of how you sound. We all dislike the sound of our voice but it's important to listen to work out how we can make it even better.

Here are a few things to think about:
- What is your tone like? Does it stay on one level or are you moving it up and down?
- Pace. Are you talking too quickly? Are you varying your pace to add focus to a particular point or reflection?
- Can you add a 'Pause', giving you a chance to slow down and draw the listener in?

- Are you adding any filler words such as 'like', 'you know', etc? These can become distractions.

What is your body doing? Once you've recorded yourself, turn the sound off and watch it at a faster speed. It's a great way to see whether you have any body movements that could be off-putting.

Here are a few important things to think about:
- Are you making eye contact?
- Are you smiling? This will help build rapport and reduce nerves
- How's your handshake? Make sure it's strong enough
- How are you sitting? A solid way to sit is by having both feet flat on the floor and your knees bent. This stops your legs from shaking and you have a flat lap to put your hands on too
- What are your arms doing? Are you gesturing appropriately?
- Distractions could be fiddling with jewellery, your hair, a pen or tapping your hands. If you put your hands in your lap, it will be easier to keep them still.

Testimonial

"Once Charlie explained what employers
were looking for, it was so much easier
to describe my own experience. Also,
that really helped with my CV."
Student. Interview Coaching

Chapter 7 | Conclusions and Reflections

The Importance Of Reflection

Finally, a reminder that taking the time to reflect allows you to slow down, just long enough, to make the most of your learnings.

"Reflection – Looking back so the view looking forward is even clearer"

Unknown

We suspect that some of you will have seen the word 'Reflection' and thought about moving on. If we lead with high extroverted energy, our need to go fast could stop us from reflecting and therefore maximising our learning.

'When F1 cars are in a race, they slow down as they enter a bend, this means they can accelerate out of the bend still in control. Sometimes we need to slow down so that we can go fast.'

So What?

What have you learnt in this Book about preparing for an interview?

What THREE things stand out to you from reading Chapters One to Six that will help you interview with impact?

Write them down. If you write them down, you are more likely to remember to act
on them.

To End

*"An interview should be looked forward
to; it's an opportunity for students to show
the best of themselves and to demonstrate
why they are a suitable candidate."*

Teacher. Clayesmore School.

You now have the understanding and knowledge to be confident in who you are and what you do, so you can be proactive, confident, and articulate when preparing, practising, and performing in an interview.

We wish you the best of luck.

AND REMEMBER <u>to complete your Challenge</u>

For anyone who emails me their 'Tell Me About Yourself' sentence, you will be put into a quarterly drawer to win a C-Me Report for themselves or a family member. We shall also share some feedback to help you make it even better.
Email your sentence to hello@flyingstartxp.com

BOOK THREE: WHICH WAY NOW?

How To Navigate Your Way into the World of Work

Contents

01. Awareness
02. Confidence = Employability
03. Resilience

Introduction

Why Are You Here?

In Book 1: Here I am, you started your journey, looking at who you are, and understanding your Native Genius. You looked at how your hobbies, your skills, your behaviour preferences, and your values give you:

- A greater understanding of the strengths you have
- A language to help you articulate these strengths
- The knowledge of the environments in which you'll thrive
- An understanding of the types of work that will energise you.

If you haven't read this book, head to 'Here I am' Book 1 in our FSXP eBook series.

We know that the world of work is changing rapidly, and after reading Book 1, you will have the knowledge, understanding and awareness to help you succeed and be happy in this changing environment, choosing the right path for you.

How do you start building that path? What direction should you take? University, an apprenticeship, a degree apprenticeship? A year out?

What path will work for you?

At Flying Start XP we have a passion for understanding your 'Native Genius', this was our whole focus in Book 1. Knowing your Native Genius is the starting block for you to know where in the workplace you thrive. With this knowledge, you will have the language to help you choose and make your own path, confidently.

At Flying Start XP, our focus is to Enable Employability, we help you unlock your Native Genius so you can succeed in the world of work. Since our foundation in 2016, we believe that if you know more about yourself, your natural strengths, and what's important to you – what makes your heart sing, this is the key to unlocking your next steps and to finding and securing the right role for you.

But what is the right role for you? How do you know? Where do you even start?

Whether you are at school, at university or starting your business career, this book is here to help you discover what's out there, your career choices and how to create a network and opportunities for yourself, setting you firmly on the path to career success.

Start With The End In Mind

By the end of this Book, you will know more about the world of work, how your Native Genius fits and where you can add value to an organisation. You may even have more focus on what you want to do and how you're going to achieve it.

To make the most of this Book, we thoroughly suggest you note things down, either in your notebook you started using for Book 1, a new notebook or create an online folder so you can keep everything in one place: the outcomes of the exercises, the learnings, the commitments, and anything else that springs to mind as you're reading this book.

Enjoy our FSXP 'How To' series supporting more young adults who want successful and happy working lives.

Book 1: Here I Am: How to Unlock Your First Career. Discovering your natural strengths, skills, and behaviours. For School Leavers and Graduates

Book 2: Look at Me! How to Interview with Impact. For School Leavers and Graduates

Book 3: Which Way Now? How to Navigate Your Way into the World of Work. For School Leavers and Graduates

Book 4: Can You Hear Me? How to Build Confidence

in the Art of Communication. For School Leavers and Graduates

Take this opportunity to challenge yourself, reflect and act.

Enjoy!

Alex

Testimonial

"Charlie's passion for helping others is so eminently obvious from the first second that you begin to speak with her. Her excitement as she guides you and allows your brain to find the right answers is very hard not to replicate, and I truly feel more ready and eager to tackle my future after just a short conversation - her energy is exactly what I needed to stop procrastinating, clear the rust in my brain, and get to work! Her knowledge of business is matched by her understanding of the human mind, how to communicate with different individuals and help them to answer their own questions, rather than simply thinking and speaking for them."
1:1 Graduate Coachee – Re-energising the Job Hunt

Chapter 1 | What's Out There?

Future Of Work

The Future of Work is changing.

Did you know that 'Artificial intelligence (AI) will automate 7 million jobs over the next 20 years?' This was a statistic shared by PwC back in 2019.

The good news is, they also revealed that AI will also create 7.2 million jobs.

Surely that's exciting!

Have a look at this video, it brings to life the Future of Work for you to see. Click here to watch https://flyingstartxp.com/go/future

How did you feel after watching that? Nervous? Excited?

AI is coming, and AI will continue to adapt the way we work. We need to be adaptable and ready for these changes. We just need to know how we prepare for that.

(If you want to learn more about AI and the Future of Work, head to our Book: AI and the Future of Work: How to support our young adults navigating this new world – Coming Soon)

Introduction

Here's a statistic we love to share...

> '85% of the jobs that will exist in 2030
> haven't even been invented yet'
> Institute for the Future (this was
> stated back in 2018)

This highlights even more, the importance of soft skills, or human skills as they are often referred to, knowing who you are and what you can do, gaining confidence and being proactive in an organisation. It's these skills which will open doors for you.

Continuum Of Certainty

Many of you will have been asked, many times 'So what do you want to do when you leave school?'. It's frustrating when you don't know but it is one of the quickest ways for someone to understand more about you, pick up on your interests, start a conversation and possibly help you.

We, adults, love to help!

Some of you will know exactly what you want to do, and others may not have a clue. If you had to rate your answer between 1 and 10, what would it be?

- 1 means – I have no idea whatsoever of

what I want to do, I'd rather hide in
- a cupboard because of the pressure
- or 10 – I know exactly what I want to do, get out of my way so I can reach my goal!!

I want you to think of the number that relates to you.

Those at the lower end, ask yourself 'What don't I want to do?'

Story - Summer Holidays

In the summer holidays after A levels, I worked in my dad's office. He is an accountant. It taught me so much. It taught me that I didn't want to work in a dull, quiet office where there was little people interaction. I needed light and colour and lots of people and activity. All my jobs since have been in companies full of colour, fun, laughter, great teams and doing exciting work. Not that I knew it at the time, but it taught me what I didn't want to do.

Maybe you have some experiences like this to draw upon. If you haven't, go and get some.

Those who are at the top end of this continuum, ask yourself
- What are your next steps to getting to your goal?
- Have you had work experience in that field?

- Who do you know in that field that would be interesting to talk to?

I'm now going to tell you a short story of my journey as I want it to show two things which I'll highlight at the end.

Story - Squiggly Career

When I was 13, I was asked the same question, 'what do you want to do'. I was lucky, I was in the ten position as I knew I wanted to be a PE teacher as I loved my sport. I had an awesome PE teacher who was a great role model and I'd always helped coach. I was working a Saturday job in a sports shop, and everything I was doing focused on my love of sport, it seemed a natural fit but, when I got there and I was doing it, I thought, actually I want to do something different, this doesn't satisfy me.

A few of the jobs I've had since are:
- Working on a Channel 4 TV sports show
- Looking after the top 20 surfers of the world – who knew that job existed!
- Working at Wimbledon
- Project Manager for corporate events
- Directing large events for Sky TV, National Geographic, Umbro (England Football Teams Kit Launches)
- Working with a Dragon from Dragons Den
- Helping technology companies tell a better story about the products they have

invented

- And now... a Leadership Consultant optimising individuals and teams to be high performers

What this means is that you are going to have many jobs, so it doesn't matter if you don't get it right the first time. I was at a ten but when I got there, I went down to a six (as I knew I wanted to work in sports). After having children, I then went down to a four, I had no idea. I am now back up to a ten.

People talk about a Portfolio or Squiggly Career. To help you find out the type of career you'd like to aim for, you have to get out there, test the market, and see what you like and what you don't like. Get experience, as this not only gives you insights but also more skills which you can talk about in an interview.

We call this the ABCD* of work.

A – Get A Job
B – Get a Better Job
C – Get a Career
D – Get your Dream Job

*This acronym comes from the wonderful Bob Clewley who was working with us at The Princes Trust at the time. We continue to use it because it's so simple and can take the pressure off finding that Dream Job so quickly. Thank you, Bob.

My second point is that I had no idea any of these jobs existed when I was at school. Half the jobs you'll end up doing haven't even been invented yet. The world of work is so exciting - get out there and see what doors open for you. Be flexible. Just give it a go. When it doesn't work out you still win because you learn so much and have more stories to tell! This is called experience.

So how can this Book support you in finding out a little more about what the world can offer?

Industry Sectors

First, let's explore the Industry Sectors out there.

There are so many sectors that you can work in. How many on this list fill you with joy? And this is by no means all the sectors - a bit of research will give you some more.

- Aerospace
- Agriculture
    - Fishing
    - Timber
- Automotive
- Chemical
    - Pharmaceutical
- Computer
    - Software
- Construction
- Defence

- Arms
- Education
- Energy
- Electrical
- Entertainment
- Financial Services
  - Asset Management
  - Banking
  - Insurance
  - Investment
- Food
- Health Care
- Hospitality
- Manufacturing
  - Steel
  - Shipbuilding
- Mass Media
  - Broadcasting
  - Film Industry
  - Music
  - News Media
  - Publishing
- Telecommunications
- Transport

If you know the industry you want to work in start speaking to people in that industry and find out more about it. Questions could be as simple as:

- What do you love about the industry you work in and your role?
- How did you get into it?

- What are your biggest challenges working in this industry?

Maybe you can start to get some work experience within the industry – more stories to tell and more experience to add.

What happens if you don't know what industry you want to go into? What about looking at the different roles you can play within each sector? Maybe you want to be an accountant, social media expert or HR manager. You can do that in any industry.

Let's share some of the most basic roles within a business.

Accounting & Finance

- Preparing management accounting information and analysis to help managers to plan, control and make decisions
- Financial record keeping of transactions involving monetary inflows or outflows
- Preparing financial statements for reporting to external parties such as shareholders
- Calculating any tax due on business profits
- Paying wages and salaries and maintaining appropriate income tax and national insurance records.

Production

- Production planning and scheduling
- Control and supervision of the production workforce
- Managing product quality (including process control and monitoring)
- Maintenance of plant and equipment
- Control of inventory
- Deciding the best production methods and factory layout.

Human Resources Management

- Ensuring that the right people are recruited for the right jobs
- Enabling employees to carry out their responsibilities effectively and make use of their potential
- Negotiations over-pay and conditions
- Dealing with complaints from employees or the employer
- Making sure employees work in a healthy and safe environment
- Deciding on redundancies and agreeing on redundancy payments.

Purchasing / Procurement

- Acquire goods and services for use by an organisation
- Buying goods and services for the entire organisation (not just for the production function, i.e. office equipment, computer

equipment)
- Negotiating buying goods and services, establishing the best price with quality and supplier reliability.

Marketing & Advertising
- Research to discover the needs of its customers
- Having the right product in terms of benefits that customers value
- Developing product packaging, pricing, and creative materials for informing potential customers of the company's offerings
- Setting the right price consistent with potential customer's perception
- of the value offered by the product
- Making the product available in the right place at the right time – including choosing appropriate distribution channels.

Research & Development
- Developing new products or processes and improving existing products/ processes
- Providing exactly what its customers want in the most efficient, effective, and economical way.

Administration & Management
- Chief Executive Officer (CEO), and any

other managers involved in making decisions for the company are a part of the administration department.

- Managers oversee employees and implement company directives created by the CEO.
- Managers can interview and hire new employees for the company.

Sales

- Needed in companies that sell retail or wholesale items to other businesses or consumers
- Build customer relationships, meet particular revenue goals and pitch new products; call, email or visit prospective customers.

IT

- Communication tools between employees, suppliers, and customers
- Managing inventory to track the quantity of each item a company maintains
- Data Management of documents and information for the whole company
- Management Information Systems to track sales data, expenses, and productivity levels
- Customer Relationship Management systems (CRM) capture every interaction a company has with a customer, helping to manage customer service

- Cyber Security.

Those of you who know what role you want to do, then you may be suited to a larger company that has a good team in this department so you can learn everything you need to know about this one role. Those who like the idea of a few of the roles may find a small or medium company a better bet because you're more likely to experience lots of different roles in one job due to a smaller amount of people.

- Large company v small company?

- Slow-paced company v fast-paced company?

- Working in an office v working at home?

- Working within a team v working mainly on your own?

By answering some of these simple questions, you begin to get nearer and nearer to the type of company and role that will work for you.

Work Experience

You now have three different ways of identifying what you want to do for your first role, you can look at:
- Industry
- Role or department

- The skills and strengths you have (Book 1: Here I am)

What's Next?

Let's have a look at work experience and how important this can be in getting your ideal job or next step, because choosing the right place for your work experience can increase your employability.

Story

The Director of Arts at Chichester University School for Performing Arts famously says in his introduction to potential students that if he found that they had a part-time job working in Tesco, he would find an excuse to go down to that Tesco store and tell the store manager something bad about that person and get them sacked.

Why?

Because if you want a job in the creative arts, you should be gaining work experience in theatres, art galleries, and singing in old people's homes – something that is going to add direct value to your employability in that sector. You may argue that a job at Tesco will give you some skills that may be beneficial in the arts, for example – interacting with the general public, learning how people act and behave BUT, he would argue, that there are far better ways to gain the skills required. It's about being seen in the right place, networking for future use and being in the place you want to work.

Work Experience – What Will It Be?

Don't worry if you still don't know what you want to be doing, many people in their 40s and 50s still don't know. The key thing is to keep moving forward and remember the ABCD of jobs and the squiggly career.

Here are a few more helpful questions to help you think about the type of role you may enjoy whether that be Work Experience or your next paid venture. As you ask yourself these questions, stop and visualise yourself at work.

- Where would you ideally be living? Home, abroad, friends, a big city, don't mind?
- Are you being paid?
- Who are you working with? Family, friends, loose connections, young people, kids…?
- How are you travelling to work – tube, bike, bus?
- What is the size of your organization? Corporate, small, fast-paced, young?
- Working alone or in a team?
- What size of the team?
- Outdoors or indoors?
- What type of culture e.g., fast, and furious, creative, competitive, supportive?

Just by reflecting on some of these questions, you'll start to figure out what environments you like to thrive within. And remember your C-ME™ blend of colours (from Book 1: Here I am) and what your two top colours may say about the type of work you'll enjoy. Understanding your Native Genius will be of huge help when answering the above questions.

If you've not yet read it, we highly recommend you do because the next chapter is all about connecting your C-Me™ profile with the workplace. Check out Book 1: Here I am.

Testimonial

"Flying Start XP is a really engaging way to prepare anyone for the rapidly changing future of work. Their course is the perfect way to learn how to make the most of any opportunities that will arise in life. "
George. Pupil. 3-day Future Leaders Programme

Chapter 2 | What's the Right Work Environment for You?

So how do you pull everything together and apply it to your next steps, to your career?

We have looked at your strengths (Book 1: Here I Am) and you've had a chance to think about where you have used these strengths, and questioned whether they really are your strengths and whether they energise you when you're doing them?

You've understood your behaviour preferences in more detail and the difference between Extroverted and Reflective behaviours and Thinking and Feeling. You've had a chance to look at your skills, what skills come naturally and where do you need to invest time in growing the skills? Are your skills the same as your strengths? We've even had a glimpse into your values, what drives you and your behaviours.

Taking time to slow down and focus on yourself, can be so important when you're focusing on where you're going next.

So how does all this help?

Understanding How Knowing Your Strengths And Skills Can Help You

If you spent 35 hours a week working, that would be 1,795 hours per year and over 84,365 hours in a lifetime. Of course, this depends on your role and the industry you work in, but you get the idea. We all need to make sure we're doing something that energises us and not depletes and drains us.

We can't expect to be energised all the time; we must graft; we must put the effort in.

Understanding How Knowing Your Behaviour Preferences Can Help You

Let's head back to C-Me™ for a moment.

Knowing more about your C-Me™ profile and behaviours, when investigating industries and different roles, will be of huge help to you because you can start to understand the types of environments in which you will thrive.

Let's describe a few company C-Me™ wheels.

For each company, I shall describe where the majority of people in that company sit on the C-Me™ wheel. Can you match the industry to the right company wheel?

1. Company Wheel One: The majority of the people sit in Green / Yellow part of the

    wheel

2. Company Wheel Two: The majority of people sit in the Red / Yellow part of the wheel with a splattering in the blue

3. Company Wheel Three: The majority of people sit in the Green / Blue part of the wheel

4. Company Wheel Four: The majority of people sit in the Yellow part of the wheel

Note: For the full images, head to www.flyingstartxp.com/resources/books and download the pdf version.

The industries to match them against are:-

- Restaurant / Bar
- Pharmaceutical
- Estate Agents
- Primary School Teachers

(Answers to be found at the end of the book – how many did you get right?)

C-Me™ Overview (Remember You Are A Blend Of All Colours)

Different industries will offer different working environments and we all thrive in different environments. Those with higher extroversion may prefer a faster pace than those who lead with reflection. Slow and steady is often a preferred environment for them. Those leading with Thinking may choose an industry that links with problem-solving and logic compared to those who lead with feeling, people are key for them to enjoy their role.

Sector

When thinking about the type of role you may want to do, consider your strengths and C-Me™ behaviours.

For those with high extroversion, you'll more than likely thrive in a role which has a faster pace, and those with high reflection will more than likely thrive at a slightly slower pace. (Remember you are a blend of all colours though)

- High Yellows will love innovation, creativity, new ideas, fun, communication, people
- High Reds will love making decisions under pressure, making the sale, doing a big deal
- High Greens will love working in teams, supporting others, a lower level of pressure
- High Blues will love getting into the detail, using their logic, and slowing things down to get it right

Just understanding your behaviour preferences, may start to guide you to the type of work you will enjoy doing, the environments in which you will thrive and the industries you'd like to work within.

Values

Companies spend a lot of money focusing on their values. As you know from our earlier exercise in Book 1: Here I am, values are what drive behaviour. They are our compass for how we are to interact, communicate and make decisions within our roles.

If you know the values of a company, that will help you understand whether you will thrive in that culture.

When you see a job or company that excites you, whether it's the industry or the role, it's worth researching what the company's values are. How close are they to yours? Will their values and culture allow you to live your values? Does the company itself live their values?

These further insights into how companies behave on a day-to-day basis will give an even greater understanding of the type of work you gravitate towards.

Here are just a few examples of the types of roles you may know about and the colours they align well with.

Note: Remember though, you are a blend of colours and only you know whether the roles could energise you.

For example, you may want to go into Medicine. Medicine is a huge subject with different strengths needed depending on your role.

- A medic with high red may enjoy A&E or the pressure of being a top-class surgeon
- A medic with high green may enjoy a GP surgery or being in a ward where more care and attention can be given to patients.

In the same industry, different colour preferences are required.

To follow is a <u>very top-line view</u> of some of the jobs that could work well for different colour preferences. <u>Please note though that the environment is the most important thing</u>, the below list may give you some further ideas but it's not conclusive, it's just there to help you get your thought process going. For example, you can be a Lawyer if you lead with any colour, the environment in which you will thrive will be different though depending on your colour blend.

COLOUR Me: Jobs

High **Blue** Preference
- Auditor
- Accountant
- Chief Financial Officer
- Web Development engineer

- Government Employee
- Civil Engineer
- Economist
- College Professor
- Data Communication Analyst
- Emergency Room Physician
- Investment Banker
- Personal Financial Adviser
- Software Developer
- Computer Programmer
- Software Designer
- Financial Analyst
- Economist
- Executive
- Architect
- Economist
- Pilot

High **Red** Preference

- Insurance Sales Agent
- Pharmacist
- Lawyer
- Project Manager
- Politician/Political Consultant
- Management / Business Analyst
- Advertising Creative Director
- Market Research Analyst
- Venture Capitalise
- Entrepreneur
- Property Developer
- Marketing Director
- Entertainment Agent
- Sports Coach

- Executive
- Lawyer
- Judge
- Detective
- Banker
- Investor

High **Yellow** Preference

- Actor
- Teacher
- Social Worker
- Sales Manager
- Sales Representative
- PR Account Executive
- Child Welfare Counsellor
- Interior Designer
- Environmental Scientist
- Advertising Executive
- Public Relations Specialist
- Corporate Coach / Trainer
- Employment Specialist
- HR Professional
- Nurse / Healthcare Worker
- Hairdresser
- Customer Relations Manager

High **Green** Preference

- Dentist
- Librarian
- Franchise Owner
- Fashion Designer
- Physical Therapist
- Massage Therapist

- Landscape Architect
- Social Worker
- Shopkeeper
- Psychologist
- Writer / Editor
- Secondary School Teacher
- Therapist / Mental Health Counsellor
- Customer Service Representative
- HR Diversity Manager
- Organisational Development Consultant
- Graphic Designer
- Physical Therapist
- HR Development Trainer

Reflections

Here's a chance to reflect and add some thoughts to your notebook

- What industries and roles stand out to you and why?
- What strengths and skills can you bring to this role?
- Do you feel energised just thinking about it?

Testimonial

"Charlie could not have been more supportive. After being on the hunt for over 10 months and applying for over 60 jobs, she provided me with such relevant advice and guidance that saw me land my dream role within two weeks of our first chat. If you are a young person who needs a helping hand or is feeling a little bit lost in the current job market, I could not recommend her services more."

Graduate 1:1 Coaching - Job-hunting.

Chapter 3 | Broadening Your Horizons Using Your Networks

Introduction

Your networks can be key to supporting you in finding work experience, knowledge and contacts to support you in your ABCD journey of work. The more people you can chat with, the more you will find out and the more opportunities will come your way.

We have two types of networks:
- Closed Networks: those people we know well and have a similar background to us. Examples – family members, school friends, club mates (music, drama, sports)
- Open Networks: those people we know that come from a variety of areas of our lives. We may not see them a lot. Examples – extended family, family friends, teachers, school/club acquaintances, colleagues from work experience

A great exercise to do is to write a list of everyone you know in your Closed Network and your Open Networks – yes this could take some time. The aim is that you can start to see who could support you in your next steps.

Think of the work experience you've had; how did you get it? Did it come from someone in your closed network or open network? Or neither?

Maximising Your Networks

Some of you will already be using your networks which is great, but I bet your networks can work even harder for you moving forward So how can we help you grow your networks?

Being Curious

'To be interesting, you have to be interested'

Dale Carnegie, Author of 'How to Win
Friends and Influence People.

This quote is a great reminder that we must be curious, we have to be interested in others, interested in situations, and just interested full stop. If we have curiosity, we will ask more questions and when you ask more questions, you learn more stuff!

It's not rocket science.

On a scale of 1 to 10, how curious are **you** about the world of work?

Where Do 'Chats' Lead You?'

The more curious you are, the more chats you have
and look what could happen
when you have lots of chats.

Step 1: Networking is about having lots of chats
Step 2: The more chats you have, the more
opportunities you create...
Step 3: Work Experience
        Volunteering
        Internships, and this helps develop...
Step 4: Increased Skills
        Broadening of Experiences
        Wider Networks, which enables you to
    build...
Step 5: A better CV / Linkedin Profile
Step 6:Greater chance of an interview and more
stories to tell at interview
Step 7:More likely to find your ideal role

*"Become friends with people who aren't
your age. Hang out with people whosefirst
language isn't the same as yours. Get to
know someone who doesn't come from
your social class. This is how you see
the world. This is how you grow"*

Quote Courtesy of Bethan Richmond. Capgemini

Challenge

From your list of people in your networks, your challenge is to chat with three people from your Closed Networks and three people from your Open Networks and be curious about their work. How they got there, what they love, what they find frustrating and what their day-to-day job looks like.

People LOVE talking about themselves.

We've even given you a list of questions you could ask them.

- What do you do?
- How did you get to be doing what you do?
- What are your day-to-day jobs?
- What are your biggest challenges at work?
- What frustrates you about your job?
- What advice would you give to your 17-year-old self?
- Do you wish you had chosen another career, if so what and why?
- Are there any opportunities you had that you wish you had taken?

Testimonial

"The highlight of Cranleigh Careers has to be our Futures Week with Flying Start XP. They put our lower sixth formers through their paces with a plethora of activities from personal impact; body language and social media workshops; negotiating tasks; team dynamics and challenging interviews. Pupils are now equipped with essential tools and top tips to support them in their search for their future. The facilitators were highly professional, approachable, and knowledgeable – a pleasure to work with."

Amanda Reader, Head of Careers at Cranleigh School

Chapter 4 | Basic Linkedin & Guerilla Tactics to Find a Role

Introduction

How do you use social media? What are you posting? What platforms are you using?

How do employers use social media? What are they looking for?

I think it's safe to say that most people are on social media, both employees and employers.

How do HR professionals use social media?
- Employers will use your social media accounts to find out who the real you is
- They want to know more about your values, that you're ethical and won't
- embarrass the company

On a scale of 1 – 10 (ten being 'I'm amazing and my social media provides a positive reflection of who I am,' to one, being 'I'm too ashamed!'), how would you score yourself out of 10?

The next step could be 'what can I do now to make my social media a more positive reflection of me. Maybe over the coming weeks can you think about how you can change or if you need to change your social media behaviour, especially if you're currently job hunting.

Linkedin

How are you using Linkedin?

Why do people use it?

Linkedin shares your skills, shows that you're serious about working and it's the new form of CV. It also helps build your professional brand and expand your professional network in general.

Your Linkedin profile allows you to show
- A photo
- Your present role
- Occupation
- Overview where you can add more about yourself, what you've done, what you're doing and what your passions are. This is your Personal Statement, but you have more space.
- Articles you've written or commented on
- Experience
- Education
- Awards, volunteering, skills
- Recommendations
- Groups

Your Linkedin profile gives you A LOT of space and opportunity to shout from the rooftops about all the amazing things you've done and experiences you've been involved in. Whether it's volunteering, work experience or paid work. There is even space for those people you've worked with to write a recommendation too. After every work experience or volunteering – get them to recommend you via Linkedin. There is even a Top Tips for students' section on Linkedin too.

Did you know that keeping your positions up to date on Linkedin makes you **18 times** more likely to be found in searches by members?

But how do recruiters use it?

- There is a specific 'recruiters' package' on Linkedin that you can't see but it allows them to search for candidates using keywords
- This is called the Boolean Search which is an algorithm which pulls up people's Linkedin pages / CVs which include certain words, skills and the experiences the job requires

Example

If a recruiter was looking for someone wanting an internship who was organised, goo at time keeping and a great communicator. They would put into the search 'internship' and 'organised' and 'timekeeping' and 'communication.'

All profiles that mention ALL of these four skills will come up and those are the ones the recruiter will read. If they wanted only two or three of these skills, then they would search 'internship' or 'organised' or 'timekeeping' or 'communication.'

As you would imagine, a lot more CVs would be pulled up.

So What?

When writing your Linkedin Page and your CV, if you have three strengths/skills you are brilliant at (Remember Book 1: Here I am) make sure these skills are in your CV and on your Linkedin Page more than once, as then you'll be higher up the list when using the Boolean search.

OR if you see a job you want, and they've highlighted the skills required, ensure these skills are in your Personal Statement as well as in the body of your CV and Linkedin profile.

There are many blogs online which advise you about how to build the best Linkedin profiles and how to use them effectively.

To learn more about Linkedin, to receive our 'FSXP Linkedin Top Tips, email us at hello@flyingstartxp.com using the title 'Linkedin Top Tips.

Creating a Linkedin profile shows that you mean business and you understand the power of the network.

Guerrilla Tactics

How do people naturally recruit?

Businesses recruit in this order: -
1. Networks
2. Agencies
3. Advertising

Job Hunters Search in this order: -
1. Advertising
2. Agencies
3. Networks

To help find a job quicker, you need to find the Sweet Spot ie The Networks

Story

When I started in business, I wanted to get into sports events. So, I looked up all the sports companies and called them up. I asked them who their Temping Agencies were. I then called up the top, most suggested Temping Agencies and registered on their books. I not only got work within sports companies, I also got a lot of experience in the different ways they ran. I ended up at one place, loved it, they loved me, our values connected and that became my first job after teaching.

How do you get into the Sweet Spot?

- Parents or family connections (your networks)
- Writing blogs on social media – be interesting
- Finding people you find interesting and commenting on their work
- Offer your skills for free in companies you resonate well with
- Find out the temping agencies or recruitment agencies who recruit for the companies you want to work for.
- Join Linkedin groups
- Follow people on Twitter, connect via Linkedin
- Follow organisations on Linkedin

Social Media and Linkedin are other ways of networking. Use them and keep building your network.

Testimonial

"Working with Charlie has allowed me to realise my strengths and values whilst giving me such valuable advice. Charlie is extremely passionate, caring, enthusiastic and willing to help at all times. Her knowledge of Linkedin is amazing, and she really boosted my confidence in job hunting during this difficult time. I finally got the job I really wanted!"
1:1 Graduate Coachee – Linkedin and Interview skills

Chapter 5 | Conclusions and Action Planning

Reflection

"We do not learn from experience… we learn from reflection on experience"

John Dewey. American Philosopher

So What?

What have you learnt? What three things stand out to you from reading Chapters One to Four that have interested you?

How are you going to use this knowledge to support you moving forward? Take this time to reflect and write them down. You will then remember them more.

Action

What are your next steps going to be?

All the hard work and effort you put in now will certainly have the biggest impact on your lives when you use that energy to act.

Are you going to:
- Focus on your networks?

- Connect with people and find out more about their roles and companies?
- Research a variety of companies to find out their values and culture?
- Push yourself out of your comfort zone and connect with people in your open networks?
- Organise work experience?
- Consider the environments in which you will thrive?
- Create a strong Linkedin page?

Write any of the above statements in your notebooks. If you write it down, that also increases the chance of you doing it.

Research shows that if you state when you are going to do something, and you tell someone else, you're much more likely it gets done. So slow down, focus on achieving the above and highlight, realistically, when you're going to be able to achieve this. Think of the new habits you will need to be successful. Tell someone. Make it happen.

'Action without vision just passes the time.
Vision without action is merely a dream but
vision with action can change the world.'

Nelson Mandela

One Last Challenge

Let me take you to a party; it's run by your parents for all their friends.

What ONE question do you know you will be asked, as least once?

'What are you up to now?'

What's your answer to that question? Do you have one? I mean a really good answer.

Practice it.

An Example

'I'm currently studying A levels at xxx, I'm not sure what I want to do but I think I would like to study English at University with the idea of going into journalism. Don't suppose you know anyone in this field, do you?'

Or

'I'm graduating at the end of this year in xxx and I have no idea of my next steps, it's something I'm currently exploring. I'd love to know more about what you do. How did you get into that? What does that look like on a day-to-day basis?' (Remember, be interested to become interesting).

How do you think that can help you? What could happen after you've said something like this?

Let's put ourselves in the shoes of the adult – what are they thinking?

Adults always love to help, so take advantage. Who's in their network? Who can they connect you with? You just don't know.

Remember, the more chats you have the more opportunities come your way.

YOUR CHALLENGE – <u>A Chance to Win a Free C-Me Report</u>

For anyone who emails me their 'What are you up to now' sentence, they will be pu into a quarterly drawer to win a C-Me Report for themselves or a family member. We shall also share some feedback to help you make it even better.

Email your sentence to **hello@flyingstartxp.com**

Final Word

Good Luck exploring the exciting world of work and finding environments where you will thrive, being confident in the strengths you have and the skills you offer.

C-Me™ Quiz Question

In chapter Two, we asked you to connect the company C-Me™ wheels to the different sectors.

How did you get on?
1 = Primary School
2 = Estate Agent
3 = Pharmaceutical company Research and Development Team
4 = Restaurant / Bar

Testimonial

"I am so fortunate to have been introduced to Alex. Back in October, I was a university graduate feeling directionless and adrift, not knowing how to answer people asking, "so what do you want to do?", and I often found myself completely forgetting what my potential was made of. But three months down the line, the work we have put in has allowed me to regain a purpose and I now even know what I want to do as a career. It seems so simple now! I wouldn't mind betting that this will be one of the best investments I make this decade and I could not recommend Flying Start XP to anyone enough."
Tom. Graduate. 1:1 Coaching

BOOK FOUR: CAN YOU HEAR ME?

How To Build Confidence in the Art of Communication

Contents

01. Awareness
02. Confidence = Employability
03. Resilience

Introduction

The importance of communication in a world where we're surrounded by tech and robots is crucial. Knowing our own methods of communication and understanding why some people can interact effortlessly, whilst others find this hard, is key. This Book shares some simple tools and techniques to support and provide an understanding of how students can individually increase their confidence in communicating with others, providing top tips for networking and interviewing, and highlighting the importance of preparation and practice to build confidence.

- An overview of why communication is a key skill in the working world
- Discovery of why some find communication effortless and others not so
- Levels of Listening to ensure you first seek to understand
- Top Tips when networking and interviewing
- Connecting the dots and how to start now

FSXP

At Flying Start XP, our focus is to enable employability, we help you unlock your Native Genius so you can succeed in the world of work. Since our foundation in 2016, we believe that if you know more about yourself, your natural strengths, what's important to you and what makes your heart sing, it's the key to unlocking your next steps and to finding and securing the right role for you.

Whether you are at school, at university or starting your business career, our courses and coaching unlock your natural potential and set you firmly on the path to career success. And now we're bringing you this content in a series of books. This way, we can reach more young adults who want successful and happy working lives.

Enjoy our FSXP 'How To' series supporting more young adults who want successful and happy working lives.

Book 1: Here I Am: How to Unlock Your First Career. Discovering your natural strengths, skills, and behaviours. For School Leavers and Graduates

Book 2: Look at Me! How to Interview with Impact. For School Leavers and Graduates

Book 3: Which Way Now? How to Navigate Your Way into the World of Work. For School Leavers and Graduates

Book 4: Can You Hear Me? How to Build Confidence in the Art of Communication. For School Leavers and Graduates

Take this opportunity to challenge yourself, reflect and act.

Ready to find out how you best communicate?

Enjoy

Alex

Chapter 1 | Importance of Communication for EQ

Why Is Knowing Your Skills Important?

'You get hired for your hard skills and promoted for your soft skills.'

Simon Sinek 2022.

Hard skills are your exams and your qualifications. Soft Skills are your human skills, your ability to communicate with others, your ability to perform in a team and to know the value you bring in a group situation.

Each year, the World Economic Forum shares the top skills that employers are looking for. Here's how the lists have changed in the last 10 years.

2015
1. Complex problem solving
2. Coordinating with others
3. People management
4. Critical thinking
5. Negotiation
6. Quality control
7. Service orientation
8. Decision making
9. Active listening
10. Creativity

2020
1. Complex problem solving
2. Critical thinking
3. Creativity
4. People management
5. Coordinating with others
6. Emotional intelligence
7. Decision making
8. Service orientation
9. Negotiation
10. Adaptability and flexibility

2025
1. Analytical thinking and innovation
2. Active learning and learning strategies
3. Complex problem solving
4. Critical thinking and analysis
5. Creativity, originality, and initiative
6. Leadership and social influence
7. Technology use, monitoring and control
8. Technology design and programming
9. Resilience, stress tolerance and flexibility
10. Reasoning, problem-solving and ideation

These Top Skills showcase how important having both hard skills and soft skills/human skills are. There is a balance between relationships, getting the best from others and being able to lead so that people will follow you AND being analytically aware, using data to complex problem solve.

Which skills do you currently have?

What would you say are your top 3?

How are you using those skills now?

Have you included these skills in your CV or Linkedin profile?

Knowing your skills and being able to articulate them, especially in an interview setting, will be of great advantage to you when looking for and interviewing for a role that you want.

Times are changing (see below) as we move into the Fourth Revolution. Having greater awareness of what we do effortlessly will support us greatly at this time.

A Time For Softer Skills

18th Century – Agricultural Age (farmers)
19th Century – Industrial Age (factory workers)
20th Century – Information / Knowledge Age (knowledge workers
21st Century – Conceptual Age (concept workers) – creators and empathisers

Skills of 'High Touch': empathy, understanding subtleties of human interaction, finding joy in one's purpose Skills of 'High Concept': the capacity to detect patterns and opportunities, combine different, maybe unconnected ideas together

In this time of the Fourth Revolution or the

Conceptual Age, we need to show both High Touch and High Concept skills

- High Touch: the capacity to detect patterns and opportunities, to combine different and maybe unconnected ideas'
- High Concept: the capacity to detect patterns and opportunities, and combine different – maybe unconnected - ideas together

As the title says, it's a time for softer skills.

If we split the top ten skills that employers were looking at in 2021 into High Touch and High Concept, this is how it breaks down

Top 10 Skills in 2021

- High Touch
    - People Management
    - Co-ordinating with others
    - Emotional Intelligence
    - Decision Making
    - Service Orientation
    - Negotiation
    - Adaptability and Flexibility

- High Concept
    - Complex Problem Solving
    - Critical Thinking
    - Creativity

Every single one of the High Touch skills requires

communication.

Let's pick up on Emotional Intelligence because there is so much in here to unpick.

Emotional Intelligence

Emotional Intelligence is also known as EQ.

- Self Awareness
- Self Recognition
- Motivation
- Empathy
- Social Skill

People say that:

> *"If you are emotionally intelligent, even if you have average intellectual intelligence, you will always come out on top"*

> *Dr Neslyn Watson-Druée CBE, award-winning business coach*

Having greater EQ supports your ability to communicate in a way that brings people along with you. You have that awareness.

When we refer back to the Top Skills employers are looking for, we can see that EQ is very much needed for all of them. EQ helps you pick up on the body language of others, seeing if and when they want to contribute but don't have the confidence to do so. With greater EQ, you will notice these different cues, and support them in drawing out their ideas before they get lost or the conversation has moved on.

EQ supports problem-solving as you'll have the awareness of your strengths and those of others, ensuring that you have the right people in the room to collaborate, discuss and solve problems together. No egos, just the focus on serving the organisation, the team or the customer.

EQ is about getting the best out of others, a key ingredient for a successful leader.

Testimonial

"Flying Start XP is a really engaging way to prepare anyone for the rapidly changing future of work. Their course is the perfect way to learn how to make the most of any opportunities that will arise in life. "

George. Pupil. 3-day Future Leaders Programme

Chapter 2 | Is Communication Your Thing?

What Is Communication?

For those of you who like to know the definition behind things, here you go: Communication is 'the imparting or exchanging of information by speaking, writing or using other mediums.'

Whether you want to be a lawyer, a doctor, a researcher, a deep-sea diver, or a professional sportsman, you have to communicate your thoughts, your decisions and your findings so that others will follow.

I'm A Natural

I bet some of you are thinking, 'Communication, that's easy. I do this all the time.'

Others are thinking, 'I would rather not talk or network or put my hand up in any group situation, thank you very much!!'

At Flying Start XP, everything we do starts with self-awareness. Being aware of your ability to communicate is key. On the next page, we have given you a short activity to do which will provide you with a top-line guide as to why you believe that communication is effortless or awful. This is part of a psychometric profiling tool we use at Flying Start XP called C ME™.

For a more detailed overview of this tool, head to Book 1: Here I Am or complete your own C-Me Report by following this link www.tlrdynamics.com/c-me.

ACTIVITY

This or That

Here's a simple activity for you, to start building awareness.

When answering the questions below, think about you at work or volunteering or with your family. Whichever scenario you pick, keep thinking of that scenario all the way through.

Imagine you are standing on a line and for every set of statements below, you take one step to the left or to the right, dependent on the statement that relates to you the most. Once you have worked through the five sets of statements, where do you end up? To the left of where you started or the right? Maybe you've ended up back in the middle?

*You can also do this exercise by putting your fists out and for every question, hold out a finger on that hand depending on the statement that relates to you the most.

Statement 1
Step Left - I have a small circle of friends
Step Right - I have a large circle of friends

Statement 2
Step left - I prefer to think things through before responding
Step Right - I'm good at responding to things quickly

Statement 3
Step Left - I am better at listening
Step Right - I am better at responding

Statement 4
Step Left - In a group situation I prefer to wait to find out what other people think before giving my views
Step Right - In a group situation I like to get my ideas on the table as soon as possible

Statement 5
Step Left - If I spend the whole day with lots of people, I am exhausted and need time on my own to recover when I get home
Step Right - If I spend the whole day with lots of people, I am energised and want to talk about it when I get home

Reflection v Extroversion

These questions help us work out where we are on this spectrum of Extroverted and Reflective* Preferences. And remember this is a spectrum and you will move up and down depending on who you are with, the situation and the level of pressure. You will never be in one place all the time, but you will have a preferred starting point.

*Reflective is often called Introversion but in the work we do, we prefer to use the word reflector.

Reflector Preference:
- Observant
- Inward Focus
- Depth
- Thoughtful
- Cautious

Extraversion Preference:
- Action-Orientated
- Outward focus
- Breath
- Outspoken
- Bold

Slow Pace to Fast Pace

The question to you is

How do **extroverts** like to communicate?
- Loudly
- Quickly
- Without much thinking time
- Can change their mind

How do **reflectors** like to communicate?
- A slower pace
- Thoughtfully
- With caution
- They may not communicate as they prefer some silence to think

Think about where you are on this spectrum. This self-awareness can help you understand yourself and others too.

Here are some top tips to support you in your communication.

Extraversion Top Tips

- Learn to listen
- Don't interrupt or finish other people's sentences
- Sit on your hands
- Count to 5 before speaking
- Encourage others to speak and describe their ideas

Reflectors Top Tips

- Your thoughts are valuable – share them
- If you get interrupted, politely ask if you can finish your point
- If time is short, be aware that you might need to move to action before you would like

What can you do to build muscle in this area?

__Testimonial__

"Flying Start XP is a sure-fire way to kickstart your future! The Flying Start team were not only incredibly friendly and interesting but also helpful and keen to encourage you to pursue your ambitions."
Sixth Former. Future Leaders. 3-day Programme.

Chapter 3 | Building Communication Muscle

New Habits

In their books, '7 Habits of Highly Effective People', or '7 Habits of Highly Effective Teens', written by Stephen Covey and his son Sean Covey, the 5th Habit focuses on communication and the importance of listening first.

What does this mean?

How Do We Listen?

'You have two ears and one mouth, use them in this proportion'.

This quote is similar to Stephen Covey's Habit #5, highlighting the importance of finding out what is happening or being said before you share your thoughts.

Let's explore the different levels of listening giving us a greater understanding of how we listen.

Which level are you?

LEVEL 1: Internal listening. Listen to Speak
Listening so you can talk. Your inner voice is quite loud and you're waiting to speak

LEVEL 2: Focused listening. Listen to Understand

Listening to understand. This is where Stephen Covey wants to get you to.

LEVEL 3: Global Listening. Listen to Learn
This is when your inner voice is quiet, and you can absorb the information

Where do you think those with high extroverted preferences sit?

If you remember back to the differences between Extroversion and Reflection, we highlighted that those with high extroversion are:

- Action orientated
- Outward focused
- Like breadth and the big picture
- Outspoken
- Bold

During our workshops, we ask our students this question 'What do you appreciate about those who lead with Extroversion?' We get answers such as:

- Great at coming up with ideas
- They bring energy
- Have pace
- Happy to lead and get the project started.

We then also ask them 'What do you find frustrating about those who lead with Extroversion?' We get answers such as:

- They may not be listening
- Sometimes go with the first idea so they

can keep moving forward
- Speak before they think
- Will ask a question and then answer it themselves if it's not answered immediately.

We often talk about those with high extroversion having to think out loud. They have to extrovert their thoughts to make sense of them. When an idea comes into their head, it has to come out quickly, sometimes unfiltered!

On the opposite side of the spectrum, those who lead with reflection bring greater depth, more thought and can be more cautious. They will ask good questions to ensure things are well thought through. A frustration could be that they take too long to share their thoughts, sometimes missing the opportunity altogether.

So how does this relate to LISTENING? Let's head back to the earlier questions 'Where do you think those with a high preference for extroversion it?

Level 1

Someone with high extroversion will often have a loud inner voice, they may not be truly listening because they have thought of an idea, a solution or an action in the moment and just have to share it. Whereas someone with high reflection may have a more focused listening style. Listening to understand.

To build muscle in this area, remind yourself of our top tips from earlier

- Learn to listen
- Don't interrupt or finish other people's sentences
- Sit on your hands
- Count to 5 before speaking
- Encourage others to speak and describe their ideas

Now you are aware, you can do something about it.

Testimonial

"The highlight of Cranleigh Careers has to be our Futures Week with Flying Start XP. They put our lower sixth formers through their paces with a plethora of activities from personal impact; body language and social media workshops; negotiating tasks; team dynamics and challenging interviews. Pupils are now equipped with essential tools and top tips to support them in their search for their future. The facilitators were highly professional, approachable, and knowledgeable – a pleasure to work with."
Amanda Reader, Head of Careers at Cranleigh School

Chapter 4 | Communication Strengths

Let's Grow Some Muscle!

Communication is a muscle, it's like anything, the more you practice, the more your confidence grows.

Question: In what areas of your life will stronger communication skills help you?

Let's look at networking as a starting point.

When you are in a position where you need to network, whether this be at an interview, at a party, at a friend's house, on a bus, at a sports match or music concert, whenever you are talking to other people and engaging with others, you are networking.

The biggest network you will have currently will most probably be your school/university network. Just remember, the impact you have on people at school/university could help or hinder you as you move through life.

Let's Party

Let me take you to a party. This party is run by your parents for all their friends.

What ONE question do you know you will be asked, as least once?

'What are you up to now?' It's always asked by parents' friends who've not seen you for ages and they can't say 'haven't you grown,' anymore!

So have an answer to this question, I mean a really good answer.

In your notes, write down what your answer would be.

Here are some examples which may help you

'I'm currently studying A levels at xxx, I'm not sure what I want to do but I think I would like to study English at University with the idea of going into journalism. Don't suppose you know anyone in this field, do you?'

Or
'I'm graduating at the end of this year in xx and I have no idea of my next steps, it's something I'm currently exploring. I'd love to know more about what you do. How did you get into that? What does that look like day to day? (Remember, be interested to become interesting)

Let's put ourselves in the shoes of the adult. What are they thinking?

Adults always love to help, so take advantage.

Here's some proof of how this can work.

A young adult we worked with a few years back, practised this sentence and had it at the ready. She was invited to a friend's parents' party where she hardly knew anyone. She ended up chatting with an elderly gentleman and, he asked her that question. Her response was:

"I am currently in my second year at university, I am studying marketing and am hoping to work in sports following my degree. I don't suppose you know anyone do you?"

He happened to be the Head of Marketing for F1. He invited her in to meet the team, they loved her and offered her an internship which then led to a job once she had graduated. Bingo.

Can you see the value of being able to answer that question with confidence?

Networking can be daunting as you will be meeting and chatting with people that you don't know. If you have a few prepared sentences or sentence starters in your back pocket, this will give you greater confidence in these situations. It can be so simple.

Keep reading to find more helpful tips for when you're networking.

Testimonial

"Working with Charlie has allowed me to realise my strengths and values whilst giving me such valuable advice. Charlie is extremely passionate, caring, enthusiastic and willing to help at all times. Her knowledge of Linkedin is amazing, and she really boosted my confidence in job hunting during this difficult time. I finally got the job I really wanted!"

1:1 Graduate Coachee - Linkedin and Interview skills

Chapter 5 | Joining the Dots

Imagine a dot-to-dot puzzle which is yet to be connected. The final image is unclear.

It is this image that Steve Jobs had in mind when he said

"You can't connect the dots looking forward; you can only connect them looking back... so you have to trust that they will somehow connect in your future"

Steve Jobs

Getting out to network and practising talking to others will help you begin creating lots of dots and, as you move through your career, they will start to connect. How they connect, you will never know.

That is why it's so important to look after anybody and everybody you work with, under or manage, you just don't know when you may need their support.

Testimonial

"I am so fortunate to have been introduced to Alex. Back in October, I was a university graduate feeling directionless and adrift, not knowing how to answer people asking, "So what do you want to do?", and I often found myself completely forgetting what my potential was made of. But three months down the line, the work we have put in has allowed me to regain a purpose and I now even know what I want to do as a career. It seems so simple now! I wouldn't mind betting that this will be one of the best investments I make this decade and I could not recommend Flying Start XP to anyone enough."

Tom. Graduate. 1:1 Coaching

Chapter 6 | Building Small Talk Muscle

How many of you have avoided parties or events where you've had to speak to people you don't know? How many of you have avoided certain situations because it means you have to start a conversation without knowing anything about the other person?

For some of you, this is a safe environment, one where you come into your own. For others, it's horrendous, an environment you would rather avoid. The problem is, it's something we have to get better at. Communication is key to our success personally and professionally. The more we practice it, the easier it will become. '

How can we get better at Small Talk?

"The rehearsal is the work; the performance is the celebration of the work"

Michael Caine
(an expericnccd actor who has starred in many successful movies)

In this case, the performance = the interview!

How can we help you practice?

If you have come across the TV show First Dates,

you may remember those very awkward scenes when there is a big dip in conversation. The awkward silence.

Someone asks a question; it's answered and then more silence. Another question is asked, and they answer it, and more silence.

Your Challenge

Imagine you are at an interview, an open day, or an Assessment Centre.

You are in that position where you are meeting people you don't know and you're not sure how to break the ice. You're not sure you want to break the ice. You're quite happy on your phone!

Write down 5 questions you could ask in a situation like this.

- How far have you had to travel?
- What are you studying at the moment?
- How did you find out about the role?
- Are you nervous at all?
- I love your shoes, where did you get them?

They just need to be small talk questions.

Once you have these questions in your back pocket, it may give you the confidence to ask them.

To avoid the awkward silence, remember the very simple response **'How about you?'**

This sentence becomes your best friend. If you have been asked a question and you've given a response. Offer it back to the other person and get them to share.

Your aim is to ask enough questions and offer enough information for you to find something you both like doing and then you're away, you're in flow. If you don't give any information away for them to attach themselves to, the silences appear. You'll be talking about something you're both excited about whether that be a hobby, a destination, a subject, a movie, or a book.

TED

And once you've asked that 'What about You?' question, you can become even more curious by using TED questions as sentence starters.

T : Tell me more about that...
E : Explain to me a little further...
D : Describe to me as it sounds fun...

Testimonial

> **"This course was engaging for students
> who gained fantastic insights to help
> them with upcoming interviews. The
> opportunity to practice the skills they
> had learnt, and observe their peers in an
> interview situation, was invaluable."**
> *Penny Allen. Head of Careers.*

Chapter 7 | Building
Interview Muscle

Let's have a look at why communication is so important when you get to an interview.

You need to be able to confidently showcase who you are, your strengths and what you love and give evidence of those strengths or characteristics too. (See Book 2: Look at Me)

Communicating this with clarity, confidence and energy is key.

For those who lead with Reflection, it's about that confidence in your voice and giving some eye contact when sharing your stories.

For those who lead with Extroversion, I know you'll want to wing it, be careful as this can lead to no structure of your answers and the possibility that you will waffle.

This is why practice is so important, remember Michael Caine earlier?

The more 'chats' you can be involved in, where you can talk about yourself confidently and highlight what you're looking for, the easier it will be when you get to interview. It will feel more natural.

The Top Interview Question

Let's head to an interview now. What are they asking and how can we start building interview muscle?

Do you know what the most commonly asked question is at an interview?

'Tell me about yourself.'

If you know it's coming, make sure you have an answer for it, just like you're going to practice the question 'What are you doing now?'

For examples and more detail on creating your response, see Book 2: Look at Me.

Testimonial

"Charlie could not have been more supportive. After being on the hunt for over 10 months and applying to over 60 jobs, she provided me with such relevant advice and guidance that saw me land my dream role within 2 weeks of our first chat. If you are a young person who needs a helping hand or are feeling a little bit lost in the current job market, I could not recommend her services more. "
Graduate 1:1 Coaching - Job-hunting Graduate

Chapter 8 | How Can Communnication Help you Find Your Career?

So far in this book, we have started to focus on how communication can help us when networking, in interviews and social situations. Now let's look to see how communication can support you in finding the job of your dreams. One that will use your strengths and skills, one that fits with your values and provides an environment in which you will thrive.

Firstly, let me ask you this. Do you know exactly what you want to do?

Do you have any ideas?

Where are you on the spectrum between having No Idea to Knowing Exactly what you want to do?

Wherever you are on this Spectrum, if you know exactly what you want to do, your next step is to speak to people in that profession to find out more.

If you don't know what you want to do, you need to speak to lots of people in lots of professions to find out more. Find out what they love or find challenging in their jobs. Find out more about why they do what they do. Find out how they got into that line of work. Once you've asked lots of questions, think about whether that job or business or challenge is something you would like to do, or at least learn more about.

To help, here are a few questions you could ask.

- What do you do?
- How did you get to be doing what you do?
- Tell me about your typical day.
- What are your biggest challenges at work?
- What frustrates you about your job?
- What advice would you give to your 18-year-old self?
- If you had chosen another career instead, what and why?
- Are there any opportunities you missed that you wish you had taken?

Get yourself out there. Practice your communication skills by asking these questions and being interested in other people.

This is what will help you start laying down and creating some of those dots. And as Steve Jobs says, 'Have trust they will somehow connect in your future.' The more conversations you have with people inside and outside of your normal network, the more you talk to others, the better you'll become at communicating. Communicating builds relationships and strong relationships will lead you to success, whatever success looks like for you, not only professionally but personally too.

If you want to be

- Successful at interviews
- Successful at networking
- Successful in building relationships (work and play)
- Successful in being collaborating
- Successful in thinking of new ideas

How you communicate is key.

Testimonial

"I have recently secured an internship at a global consultancy in London. Without my course at Flying Start XP, this quite simply would not have been possible. "

Graduate 5-day Future Leaders Programme

Chapter 9 | Conclusions, Learnings and Reflections

Reflection

"Reflection – Looking back so the view looking forward is even clearer"

Unknown

I know that some of you will have seen the word 'Reflection' and thought about moving on. If we lead with high extroversion, our need to go fast could stop us from reflecting and therefore maximising our learning. Let's not miss out on this opportunity to learn.

When F1 cars are in a race, they slow down as they enter a bend, this means they can accelerate out of the bend still in control. Sometimes we need to slow down so that we can go fast.

When working with young adults, we can see how the different colour preferences approach reflection. So here are some questions that may support you.

So what?
What have you learnt? Write these in your notebook.

What 3 things stand out to you from reading Chapters 1 to 8 that have interested you?

Here is what we have covered:

- Why communication is so important in the world of work
- Our different approaches to communication: Extroversion / Reflection
- Importance of networking and some top tips
- Communication to improve your interviewing
- How a simple chat can lead to your perfect job

Write down the one action you're going to do today or tomorrow to help you build your levels of communication.

AND REMEMBER to complete your Challenge

For anyone who emails me their one action or 'Tell me About Yourself' sentence, you will be put into a quarterly drawer to win a C-Me Report for themselves or a family member. We shall also share some feedback to help you make it even better. Email your sentence to hello@flyingstartxp.com

'Great communication begins
with connection.'
Oprah Winfrey

SO GO OUT AND START CONNECTING

The FSXP Team

"Alex and Charlie are powerhouses when it comes to delivering leadership and training courses for young people. Having personally benefited from their coaching as well as collaborating with them on a leadership programme for The Prince's Trust, their energy, due diligence and expertise are inspirational and transformative! Their programme has gained the backing of a Celebrity Ambassador and is supporting hundreds of young people. I couldn't have asked for more!"
Vicky Yorke. Innovation Project Lead, Prince's Trust.

Flying Start XP has been run by Alex Webb and Charlie Welch since 2016. Alex and Charlie have a wealth of experience in working with young adults and in unlocking their full potential. Their backgrounds are mixed, and their networks cover a huge array of industry experts and amazing individuals. From education to the military to sport and entrepreneurship, Alex and Charlie get so much joy from the work they do, the content they deliver and the fun they have.

LET'S MEET THE TEAM

Alex Webb
Director, Facilitator and Coach

Alex has had a mixed career, starting as a teacher before moving into the events industry with sports TV and media, corporate and then commercial events. Following the arrival of her family, Alex worked in entrepreneurship with a focus on young technology businesses. With her roles as an Events Director and Programme Director, Alex has created, designed, and facilitated workshops, events, and programmes for an array of clients such as TfL, Innovate UK, Prince's Trust, Girls Day School Trust, Sky, Vodafone, Umbro, Lego and GSK.

As a natural mentor, Alex brings a deep understanding of the challenges facing students and graduates. To balance working with young adults, Alex is a professional facilitator and leadership consultant working with individuals and teams within the world of business to create high performance through self-awareness, resilience, and leadership. It is this work that allows her to keep her knowledge current in how businesses support and employ our young people.

Outside of Flying Start XP, Alex has also run and coached international sports teams.

Linkedin: Alex Webb (nee Spring)

Charlie Welch
Business Facilitator, Trainer, and Coach

Charlie is a leading business facilitator and programme development consultant who has worked across many business sectors. She was the first female winner of the Queen's Medal at the Royal Military Academy, Sandhurst.

Charlie has facilitated at all corporate levels,

from the boardroom to new employees and has experience nationally and internationally in public, private and not-for-profit sectors. Clients include The United Nations, EDF, Oxford and Cambridge Universities, GSK, RBS, GE, and the British Red Cross.

Linkedin: Charlie Welch

Acknowledgements

'It Takes A Village To Raise A Child'

It certainly feels a lot like this.

To be able to bring you the content of this book in the format it's in, with the exercises, quotes and order, it hasn't just happened overnight. There have been A LOT of individuals who have supported us, guided us, and given us opportunities to test out our content, activities and formats along the way. I am so grateful.

Since 2016, from starting Flying Start XP with James Prior, we have had the opportunity to build something we are proud of, from being given our first gig at the National Graduate Fair, where we made quite a stir because we were engaging, interactive and impactful from the start. This was down to the openness and sharing of some amazing people, working with Charlie Welch, the start of our FSXP relationship, Mitch Smith and Piero Vitelli, who were selfless in sharing their content so we could adapt it to this new audience.

From working with Kirsty Pank who had the hard job of cold calling large companies to tell them about what FSXP were doing and how we were 'Building the Next Generation of Business Brilliance'. Thanks so much Kirsty, it was a hard gig and completely went against your Native Genius! In our first year of trading, our focus was to be part of company graduate training schemes, so we could help them get the best from their young adults, so they could add value from day one, with heightened Human Skills in their tool kit. Actually, getting the opportunity to speak to these companies was no mean feat!!

We also focused on connecting with parents of graduates who needed advice on how to support their young adults when making that next step into business. It was at this time, we connected with Caroline Edwards and Sarah Austin who run The Really Helpful Club and were incredibly helpful (apologies for the pun!) as they brought together a group of parents who were looking for greater understanding as to how they could support their children as they moved from school to university, to work. It was here that we met Elaine Halligan, from Positive Parenting, a huge inspiration and great connection with further parents who needed support for their family members. Caroline, Sarah, and Elaine entrusted FSXP with many of their children, giving them the human skills and confidence to approach an interview and enter the workplace successfully.

It wasn't until late 2017 when Charlie and I started supporting schools, working with their Sixth Formers to build their confidence and awareness in their skills. This would then help them make better decisions about the roles they would engage well with and discover more about the environments in which they thrived. A huge thanks to Cranleigh School and The Girls' Day School Trust for believing in us and employing us for many gigs as we supported their students. We continue to work with Sixth Formers, whether that be with their Prefects developing Leadership Skills, or the whole year group, with C-Me™ Colour Profiling. Lots of fun.

2018 began our amazing relationship with The Prince's Trust, delivering our 2-day Future Leaders Programme for young adults between the ages of 16 and 30. If it wasn't for the vision and passion of Vicky Yorke, we would not have been able to positively impact as many young lives as we did over our three years relationship. Our ambassador for this programme was none other than Gareth Southgate (England Football Manager), who we had the pleasure of welcoming on the programme for one afternoon. (It happened to be the session on C-Me™ colours, a tool he uses with the England Football team).

Every Future Leaders course was supported by Capgemini. Bethan Richards and Sally Caughey could see the benefit of this programme, not only for the young adults but for the Capgemini facilitators who joined us each course to support the young adults, so they could use the learnings for their personal development too. Thanks hugely to you both. We LOVED working with you.

As our networks grew and FSXP became a recognised brand, we began to link up with the likes of Teen Tips - Well Being Hub, an incredibly inspiring, informative, and focused platform for schools, students, and parents, to support them through all the areas of worry and anxiety we may face with our young adults. Thank you to Alicia Drummond, for continuously directing parents and young adults our way so we can support them with the next stages of their lives.

Charlie and I continue to work with schools and individuals, enabling their employability and building their business brilliance and we love the work we do. With other corporate projects taking up a lot of our time, we have had to reign back the FSXP live work, which is why we wanted to ensure our content could still make an impact. The idea of writing a Book came indirectly from a family dog walk with Taylor and Gordon Drayson who I'd also like to thank. Thank you for building our colourful FSXP website and for being there to talk through ideas. You're both stars. Thank you also for a more recent connection, to Richard Crowe, our E-book designer. Thank you for taking our content and turning it into something readable and absorbable. Alongside Theo Spring whose proofreading skills and support came into play at the end of our journey, to ensure we could get this content to you, with the right grammar and spelling.

Our final thank you must go to you, for reading this book and for taking the time to focus in on you. And remember, a strong leader is one who is self-aware. You've got this.

Don't forget your challenges. I look forward to receiving your emails.

Contact Details

Alex Webb
hello@flyingstartxp.com
www.flyingstartxp.com

BOOKS IN THIS SERIES

FSXP How To Series

Introducing the ultimate guide to kick-starting your career! Our book series is tailored specifically for school leavers and graduates, providing expert advice on how to navigate the competitive world of work and build the skills you need to succeed and be happy.

In "How to Unlock Your First Career", we'll guide you through the process of discovering your passions, skills, strengths and values, helping you to choose a natural career path that's right for you.

"How to Interview with Impact," provides guidance on how to prepare for and ace any job interview. From researching the company and mastering your body language to storytelling so you make a lasting and positive impression on any potential employer or university.

Gain greater understanding of career options in Book 3 "Which Way Now: How to Navigate your way into the World of Work," a comprehensive guide that covers everything from the future of work and industry sectors to the importance of energising work and the many different career paths available to you.

And finally "How to Build Confidence in the Art of Communication," a practical guide that helps you develop your communication skills, including networking, active listening, and interviewing with confidence.

Whether you're a recent graduate, a career changer, or just looking to improve your professional skills, the Flying Start XP series, written by career expert Alex Webb, has everything you need to take your career to the next level. Don't let the competitive job market intimidate you - with our book series, you'll have everything you need to stand out and succeed!

The Ulitmate Guide To Kick Starting Your Career

A Complete Collection: The Ultimate Guide to Kick Starting your Career" is a comprehensive book offering expert advice on successfully entering the competitive world of work and building essential skills for long-term success and happiness. This invaluable resource provides school leavers and graduates with the guidance they need to make the most of their next step.

By delving into the topics of Native Genius, Strengths, Behaviour Profiling, Networking, Interviewing and Communication, this book series equips readers with the knowledge and tools necessary to navigate the challenges of starting a career, ensuring a strong foundation for a fulfilling professional journey ahead.

Here I Am: How To Unlock Your First Career

'Here I am: How to Unlock Your First Career' is a must-have resource for anyone who wants to gain a better understanding of their a career path. Written by career expert Alex Webb, this comprehensive guide provides practical advice and exercises to help readers identify their strengths, skills, behaviour preferences and values. The first in the FSXP series, where you also learn strategies for job searching, networking, and interviewing. Readers will develop the tools needed to succeed in their professional lives.

Whether you are at school, university or recently graduated, How to Unlock Your First Career is an essential read for anyone who wants to take control of their next steps.

Look At Me! How To How To Interview With

Impact

Look at Me: How to Interview with Impact for School Leavers and Graduates is the ultimate guide to landing your first job or university place. Written by career expert Alex Webb from Flying Start XP, and the second in the FSXP 'How To' Series, this comprehensive book provides practical advice on how to interview with impact. With techniques for showcasing your strengths and skills through strong storytelling, readers will have the skills needed to succeed in any interview. This book also includes tips on how to research the company, so you know what questions are coming and what questions to ask plus a template to help you analyse any job description, from this day forward.

Whether you're a school leaver, or recent graduate, this book, the second in the FSXP series, is a must-read for anyone looking to kickstart their career. With its real-world examples and easy to follow format, this book is the key to interviewing with confidence and landing your dream job.

Which Way Now: How To Navigate Your Way Into The World Of Work

Are you a recent school leaver or graduate who feels lost and unsure about your career options? Do you want to succeed but are worried about your future prospects in the competitive job market?

Look no further than 'Which Way Now', the essential guide to help you navigate the world of work.

The book is part of the FSXP 'How To' series and is packed with expert advice and practical tips on how to choose the right career path, adapt to the changing work environment, network effectively, and use LinkedIn and guerrilla tactics to secure your first job.

With 'Which Way Now', you'll have the knowledge and skills to kick-start your career and succeed in today's job market. Whether you're uncertain about which path to take or need guidance to take the next step, this book is tailored specifically for you.

Order your copy today and start your journey to a successful career!

Can You Hear Me? How To Build Confidence In The Art Of Communication

Can you Hear Me? is a practical guide for school leavers and graduates who want to build confidence in their communication skills. Written by behaviour specialist Alex Webb, and the fourth in the FSXP 'How To Series', this practical book provides readers with a framework for understanding their natural communication style, how to improve their active listening skills, and how to network and interview effectively. The book also includes real-world examples and exercises to help readers put the lessons into practice.

Can you Hear Me? is an essential resource for anyone who wants to communicate with confidence and clarity. It is a must-read for recent graduates and anyone entering the workforce for the first time.

Printed in Great Britain
by Amazon

23925047R00104